LinkedIn
for Network Marketing

How to Unleash the Power of
LinkedIn to Build Your
Network Marketing Business

Dale Moreau

LinkedIn for Network Marketing
© 2019 by Dale Moreau

CONTENTS

FOREWORD
BY TOM "BIG AL" SCHREITER

Dale Moreau is a perfectionist. Loves to make sure every detail is covered in his trainings. This book is no exception.

If you like word-for-word, step-by-step, actionable methods, then this is the book for you. Philosophy is nice, but the real work starts when we have a guideline of what to do, starting right now.

So roll up your sleeves, grab your keyboard, and get ready to make an impression on LinkedIn. Look like a pro and attract the prospects you need to build your business now.

Chapter 1:
Let's Introduce Your
Dream Builders

The difference between ten executives in your Network Marketing business and ten nonprofessionals?

LinkedIn.

LinkedIn is the social media home for professionals and executives.

Professional Network Marketers feel at home with LinkedIn. Professional Network Marketers get more traffic on LinkedIn than they get on Facebook. Twitter, Snapchat and Pinterest can't beat the power of LinkedIn.

Network Marketer #1 gives ten perfect presentations to ten perfect non-professionals on Facebook. One person joins his business.

Network Marketer #2 gives ten perfect presentations to ten perfect professionals on LinkedIn. Eight professionals join her business.

What?

People on Facebook are looking for social relationships. People on LinkedIn are looking for opportunities.

Most professionals on LinkedIn think different than other people.

- They look for opportunities.
- They make instant decisions.
- They have money to spend.
- They look for reasons why something will work.
- They ignore reasons why it won't work.
- They are problem solvers.
- They are solution givers.
- They don't procrastinate.
- They make no excuses.

Sounds like Network Marketers have the perfect home for finding leaders for their teams.

What's a better match? Network Marketers.

Most professional Network Marketers on LinkedIn think different than other people.

- They look for opportunities.
- They make instant decisions.
- They have money to spend.
- They look for reasons why something will work.
- They ignore reasons why it won't work.
- They are problem solvers.
- They are solution givers.
- They don't procrastinate.
- They make no excuses.

Notice the pattern? What professionals want are what Network Marketers on LinkedIn want.

Why? Network Marketers on LinkedIn think like professionals. Network Marketers and professionals speak the same language.

Network Marketers on LinkedIn:

- Seek other opportunities.
- Love residual income.
- Know the value of training.
- Are not afraid to buy products.
- Don't make excuses about the cost.
- Want time-freedom, financial security and health.
- Don't make promises that they can't keep.
- Know the value in sponsoring, recruiting and getting buyers.
- Are not afraid of taking risks.
- Like building rapport.
- Are open to social conversations about Network Marketing.
- Like closings and handling objections.
- Look forward listening to presentations.

Which person would you rather talk to about your opportunity, goods and services? The professional that requires lots of convincing about Network Marketing? Or, the Network Marketer who is already convinced?

The difference between a Network Marketer on LinkedIn and Facebook?

Network Marketers on LinkedIn are looking for other opportunities. Network Marketers on Facebook for the most part are not.

And the sad part? Most Network Marketers on LinkedIn fail at success. Network Marketers will make more money for being a greeter working at Walmart.

LinkedIn is the perfect place for Network Marketers to connect, recruit, and sponsor.

So, why do Network Marketers on LinkedIn fail?

- Lack of training.
- Lack of money.
- Lack of time.

The lack of training is number one for the lack of success. The lack of funds and the lack of time come from the lack of training. Train a Network Marketer with the skills for success and he will find the time and have the money.

The purpose of Network Marketing is to get "yes decisions." Lots of "yes decisions" make us lots of money. Lots of "no decisions" make us zero money. If we're not taught the skills for getting more "yes decisions" than "no decisions," our business will fail. If we can learn the skills for getting more "yes-decisions" than "no-decisions," we'll succeed.

My hope is to train you with better words for getting more "yes decisions" than "no decisions."

Network Marketers on LinkedIn are looking for other opportunities. They think like us and speak the same language as us, So, let's recruit and sponsor them.

Chapter 2:
Let's Look Smart and
Be Professional.

Your profile is your real estate. It's the first place that people see. It will either repel or attract. We'll want people attracted to our profile. So, we'll want our profile to look smart and be professional.

There are thirteen parts for a LinkedIn profile.

- Backdrop.
- Profile picture.
- Contact Information.
- Headline.
- Profile description.
- Articles and Activities.
- Experience.
- Education.
- Volunteer Experience.
- Skills and Endorsements.
- Recommendations.
- Accomplishments.
- Interests.

For this chapter, we'll work with the first four of the thirteen parts.

- Backdrop.
- Profile picture.
- Contact Information.
- Headline.

Do not neglect any one part. Use all thirteen parts for building your profile.

The rule of thumb is simple: Remove everything and start fresh and new.

If we are going to look professional, our real estate needs to look professional. Instead of Baltic Avenue, we'll need to look like Monopoly's Board Walk.

- Remove your Network Marketing company names and logos.
- Remove your regular job names and logos.
- Remove your product names and logos.
- Remove any references to looking for a job.
- Remove any work-related experiences.
- Remove all pictures resembling your products or services.
- Remove all references to universities, colleges, schools and trade schools.
- Remove all experiences with your job, your school or your trade.

- Remove all skills and endorsements not related to Network Marketing.

We'll want a clean slate starting a brand-new profile from the ground up. If you have a Network Marketing profile, then scrap it. We are going to rebuild it from start to finish.

Why start from scratch? Features vs. benefits.

Most profiles speak about features. Facts make up features. They're what a thing is.

- What you do for a living.
- Descriptions about your products.
- Descriptions about experiences.
- Descriptions about your hobbies.
- Descriptions about sports.
- Ingredients in your products.
- What schools you have attended.

No one cares. I know it is painful to hear, but it needs saying.

There is one thing and one thing only everybody cares about. "What's in it for me?"

- What can you do for helping solve my problems?
- What pains can you relieve?
- What itch can you scratch?
- What festering sores can you heal?

So, what we'll want is benefits.

- How to retire early.

- How to lose weight.

- How to make sales.

- How to have a part-time job and make a full-time income.

- How to buy a new car with little money down.

- How to take vacations at discount rates.

Most of all thirteen parts of your profile will reflect benefits.

(1). The Backdrop.

The backdrop is the eye-candy of your profile. It's a 1584-pixel X 396-pixel background image that makes a first impression. So, we'll want our backdrop to look smart and be professional.

Five parts for our backdrop.

- Name.

- Personal logo.

- Professional picture.

- Background.

- Slogan.

Your name should be on the backdrop. A personal logo should be the initials of your name. Do not make your personal logo anything more than the initials of your name.

A professional picture of yourself should be on the backdrop. Men should dress in a suit with tie and hair and beards trimmed. A professional picture should be on a white background. This allows the graphic designer to work with the image on the backdrop without too much problem.

Women should be in a nice work dress or pant suit with hair, lipstick and eye brows made. A professional photographer should shoot a picture of her against a white background.

The backdrop should be a professional background made by a professional designer. If you do not know how to make a backdrop, do not make it yourself. You can get a professional designer for reasonable prices at **Fiver.Com**.

The slogan? This is the place for our first benefit. Make it a short statement. Describe how our Network Marketing niche can help solve people's problems.

Don't know how to write a slogan? I'll show you.

Write down all the benefits for your business and products.

- A new car.
- Free vacations.
- A new home.
- Lose weight.
- Renew the mind.

- Lower electricity bill.

- Lower cell phone bill.

- Toxic free cleaners for the home.

- Lifestyle bonuses.

- Retire in 5 years.

- Work part-time at full-time wages.

- Get healthy.

- Proper nutrition.

Now we are going to add our benefits into a formula. "**I show people how to…**" + "**A Benefit**."

- I show people how to get a new car each year without paying for it.

- I show people how to take five-star vacations at one-star prices.

- I show people how to get a new home without a mortgage or monthly payments.

- I show people how to lose weight without eating funny foods or exercising at the gym.

- I show people how to get a raise each month without telling the boss.

- I show people how to fuel the fire in their minds for better memory and improved learning.

- I show people how to get electric companies to pay their electricity bills.

- I show people how to lower their cell phone bills and get paid for it.

- I show people how to clean their home without toxins or harming the environment.
- I show people how to retire in 5 years at full pay.
- I show people how to work part-time with full-time wages.
- I show Network Marketers how to get more yes decisions than no decisions.
- I show people how to wear a computer-watch and stay hydrated and energized all day long.
- I show people how to get healthy and get paid big money for it.
- I show people how to get healthy and make more money part-time than they make full-time at their jobs.
- I show people how to live a healthy active lifestyle and get paid for it.
- I show people how to earn an extra income that pays them what other people cannot afford.
- I show Network Marketers how to turn their prospects' every "no-decisions" into "yes-decisions."
- I show people how to energize their bodies and stay alert during the day and calm during the night.
- I show people how to eat sixteen vegetables a day chewing one vitamin before lunch or dinner.
- I show people how to increase their lifestyle and get the IRS to pay for it.

We're not done. Another formula works its magic. **"Would it be okay if…"** + **"A Benefit"** + **"A Call to Action."**

- Would it be okay if you never had to show up at work again? Look no further!

- Would it be okay if you could drive a new car each year without making payments? Let's connect!

- Would it be okay if you could get more holiday time? Read no further!

- Would it be okay if you could get paid for living in a new home without a mortgage or payments? Look for the video!

- Would it be okay if you could burn fat 24/7? Look further but you won't find it!

- Would it be okay if you could walk away from your boss and never had to worry about money again? Seek elsewhere, but you'll only find it here!

- Would it be okay if you could refuel the mind to recover lost memories? Look no further! You've found the right place.

- Would it be okay if you could make your electricity bill smaller? Look no further.

- Would it be okay if you could get your cell phone paid in full each month? Well, you've found the place. Look no further.

- Would it be okay if you could help the environment? Well, you've found the right place. Look further but you won't find it.

- Would it be okay if you could retire in 5 years at full pay? We've got you covered. Look no further.

- Would it be okay if you could work part-time and get paid full-time? You've landed in the right place. Take time to look.

- Would it be okay if you could turn your prospects' every no decision into yes decisions? Find it here.

- Would it be okay if you could wear a tech-savvy jewelry piece to hydrate damaged and thirsty cells? Look here.

- Would it be okay if could get healthy and get paid big money for it? No need to look further.

- Would it be okay if you could get healthy and make more money part-time than you make full-time at their job? Stop Looking. You've Found the Right Place.

- Would it be okay if you could get paid for living an active, healthy lifestyle? Look no further than here.

A piece of cake, agreed? This is more fun than squeezing the neck of a ducky made of rubber. (I'm kidding. There were no rubber duckies harmed during the writing of this book).

FYI: Keep the right side of your profile clear from your mugshot, logo and slogan. Your profile picture will show up there.

(2). The Profile Picture.

The difference between an amateur Network Marketer and a professional on LinkedIn?

The profile pictures.

Have a professional photographer take a picture of you. The profile picture is 400-pixels X 400-pixels.

Whatever you choose, dress in a suit for the men with hair combed and beards clean-cut. For women, dress in a nice dress or work pants with makeup and hair done.

Your head shot should look as professional as your picture on the backdrop.

A few more things. Don't wear sunglasses. Smile, but not too much. Don't change your profile picture to black and white.

(3). Contact Information.

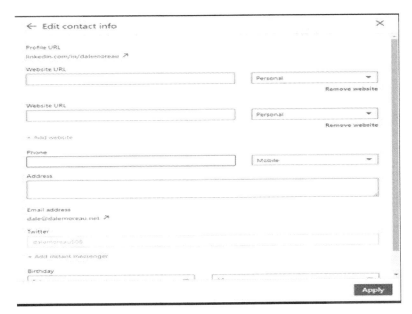

A stellar profile requires proper contact information.

- Profile URL.

- Phone Number.

- Email Address.

- Twitter and Instant Message.

- Birthdate.

The profile URL includes links for your Facebook, blogs and webpages. Don't put your link for LinkedIn. It's not necessary.

If you're in the USA, XXX-XXX-XXXX is the format for a telephone number. Use whatever format works for other countries.

Input your real email address. Do not leave this part out.

Twitter will appear when we get to the settings in a later chapter. Leave Twitter alone until then. Click "Add Instant Messenger" and input the link.

Your birthday must include the month and day of birth. The year of your birth is not required on LinkedIn. Make sure you click the "**Birthday Visible to Your Network.**" You'll want your birthdate visible.

(4). The Headline.

There are two parts of your brain. One part is logical. The other part is emotional. One part is the logical conscious mind and the other part is the emotional subconscious mind.

The emotional subconscious mind rules over the logical conscious mind. If we want to ensure our message gets through, we will speak to the subconscious mind.

So, how do people think. Words? Or, pictures? There is an old saying that a picture is worth 1,000 words. A picture can transfer 1,000 bits of information into the brain faster than words spoken.

Words speak to the conscious mind. Pictures speak the subconscious mind. Network Marketers may speak with words, but prospects think in pictures.

Would it make sense to use our skills for communicating words that paint pictures?

If we can paint emotional scenes in our prospects' heads, our message has a chance for getting through. Think of our words as the paint and the prospect's mind as the canvas.

Our headline paints a picture of what the benefits for our offers can do for people. Paint a picture of what a benefit could do, and you'll stand out for the reader. It'll be the only thing they'll remember.

Read the Word Pictures used by politicians, Hollywood and advertisers.

- "Bleeding Heart Liberal" (It pictures a person who has sympathy for the downtrodden).

- "Dark Horse" (It pictures a long-shot candidate dressed in death-march black).

- "Marilyn Monroe" (It pictures the blond, blue-eyed and sexy singer and actress of the '60's).

- "Lord of the Rings" (It pictures Frodo Baggins finding and destroying the One Ring).

- "Where's the Beef?" (It pictures a grandma opening a hamburger bun that's bigger than the hamburger patty that lays upon it).

- "Finger Lickin' Good!" (It pictures finger licking good food).

I bet these Word Pictures recalled memories when you read them. Long after the saying is gone, it stays in our minds and we don't forget.

The Word Pictures formula?

- Action Verbs +
- Adjectives and Adverbs +
- Solutions for Real Life Problems.

The number one rule for Word Pictures? Keep the Word Pictures consistent with the theme stated in the slogan of your backdrop image. And Capitalize all the major words.

List all the action verbs that describe your message. Then add adjectives and adverbs to the list. Now, picture a real-life scenario with plot-twists of characters and lots of problems. Write it in a 120-character statement for solving the problem.

Want some help? **Powerthesaurus.org**.

"Powerthesaurus.org" helps us with verbs, idioms, expressions, adjectives and adverbs. Input any word or phrase into the search engine, and it spits out powerful word pictures for our writings.

Ready for some examples? These examples may exceed 120-characters. They do give enough material for you to create your own headlines.

Weight Loss

- Melt Away Excessive Fat and Carbs. Watch Television or Play Video Games Burning Away Ugly Belly Fat.

- Eat, Sleep, Work and Play! What's missing? The Gym! No Need for the Gym with Our No-Fuss, No-Hassle Diet Plan.

- Hate the Suffering from Dieting Hunger Pains? Suffer No More. Tread where Most Diet Suffers Dare Not Tread. Lose Pounds a Day without Starving or Exercising.

- Diet While You Sleep. Dream Away those Extra "Pecan Pie" and "Apple Dumpling Pounds Sleeping in Your Own Bed.

- Lose One Pound a Day Sleeping, Working, Eating, or Playing. Try Our Calorie Killer, Cookie Cruncher Weight Loss Program Made Easy.

- Hate Cooking with All the Clean-up of Messy Dishes? Take 20-Seconds a Day and Drink Our Instant Breakfast Shake. Lose Weight while Cleaning One Dirty Glass and Spoon a Day.

- Get Slim and Thin on Pennies a Day. Drink Chocolate Shake Delights that Pleasure the Tongue and Narrow the Waist.

Cell Phones

- Your Neighbors Have Them. Your Friends Have Them. Your Family Has Them. Make Money Every

Time Your Neighbors, Friends and Family Pick Up their Cell Phones.

- Sleep, Eat, Work, and Play–The Four Activities of Life. Bills and Bank Accounts–The Two Problems of Life. Let People Talk on their Cell Phones and Make Your Bills Smaller and Your Bank Accounts Bigger. Then You Can Enjoy the Four Activities of Life.

Nutritional Products

- Microwave Fast and Oh So Delicious Breakfast Nutrition. It Slims and Trims the Waistline to Eye-Pleasing Delights. Draw Compliments from Family and Friends with One Hot Nutritious Breakfast a Day.

- Happy and Awake at 9:00 a.m. on Monday Morning but Sad and Tense at 10 a.m. on Monday Morning? That's the Other Guy. You? Happy and Awake at 6 a.m. through 6 p.m. Monday through Sunday with Our Nutrition Secret.

- The Only Person Awake at 8 a.m. is You. The Only Person Alert at Work After Lunch is You. The Only Person Calm After Work is You. Why? Because You Have the Secret to a Healthy Life.

- With Age Comes Wisdom and Better Judgment. But with Our Youth Rejuvenating Secret Comes Skin So Soft and Glowing. It Makes Your Skin Looks 16-Years Younger All Over Again.

- Dancing? Admit It. We All Would Like To. A Few of Us of a Certain Middle Age Cannot. For the "Cannots," You'll Cut a Rug and Dance A Jig after Trying Our All-Natural Yum, Yum Delicious Breakfast Meal.

Water Filters

- People Pee in their Pools. Other People Pee in Our Lakes and Streams. What Happens to All that Water? It's Recycled. Our Unit Takes Out Other Peoples' Contributions.

- Bleaching Clothes. Disinfecting the Bathroom and Kitchen. Killing Germs and Bacteria. A Great Job for Chlorine but Not a Great Job for Your Stomach. We Have the Solution.

- Clean. Crisp. Refreshing. Tasty. That's What Water Should Be. All Those Unidentified Floating Objects Turn Your Glass Dirty and Make You Sick. We Offer the Solution.

Fiber Products

- Love Pizza? Hate Rabbit Food? Love Mexican Food? Hate Hemorrhoids? Enjoy Pizza, Mexican and All Your Favorite Spicy Foods by Trying Fiber. It Takes the Ouch Out of Hemorrhoids.

- Lowering Blood Pressure is Like Deflating a Balloon with Our Tasting Fiber Supplement. Now in Snack Packs.

- Make Snacks Count. Snack on Our Fiber Supplements for a Tasty Dessert Treat Before Every Meal. Kids Love Them. Adults Approve Them.

- Jump Start Your Day with Results You Can Experience in 24 Hours.

- 15 Minutes. Take Our Perfect Diet Supplement 15-Minutes before You Eat. What Happens Next? Your Weight Problem is Gone.

Wearable Technology

- Running, Jumping, and Walking are Great Exercises. They're the First Step to Good Health. The Second Step? Having the Doctor Know You are Running, Jumping and Walking with Wearable Technology.

- Keep an Eye on Your Glucose Levels by Wearing a Watch. Fine Jewelry Worn Like a Rolex that Keeps Watch Over Your Health Like a Doctor.

- Patients Hate Doctor Visits. Doctors Hate Patient Visits. Help Fill Both Needs. One Less Visit for You and One Less Headache for Him with Our Wearable Technology.

- Patients Love It. Doctors Love It. You Ought to Love It Too. Wearable Devices that Tip Off the Doctors at the Slightest Hiccup with Your Health.

Skin Care

- Want Reflections of Perfection? Our Skin Care Makes Your Skin Look So Good that You'll Never Have to Wear Makeup Again.

- Reveal Yourself! Look 16-Years Younger All Over Again but Without the Acne.

- Touchy-Feely May Make Your Skin Crawl and You Feel Ill at Ease. That's the Tempting Nature of Those Wanting to Touch and Feel Your Smooth Skin. One Use and You'll Feel and Touch the Difference.

Organic Cleaners

- Pollution. Toxins. Keeping Your Home Safe. Which One of the Three Makes Better Sense for You?

- Harsh Chemicals Strip the Life Out of Your Floors and Furniture and Pollute the Home. Make Your Home Safe from Toxins and Chemical with Our Environmental Pleasing Products.

- Well, You Know How You Want to Help the Environment? Well, I Show People How to Stamp Out Harmful Chemicals from the Environment. Try Our Toxin Free Cleaners for the Home.

Network Marketing Opportunity

- Direct Deposit, Postal Mail, FedEx, and UPS All Have One Thing in Common. The Delivery of Extra Paychecks from Your Network Marketing Business Every Week.

- Getting Extra Paychecks for Our Business is Like Getting Paid Overtime at Your Job. Except You Don't Have to Work Twice as Hard.

- The Boss Terminator. That's What Our Business Does for You in Months and Not Years.

- Firing the Boss is Simple. You Walk in the Boss' Office and Say, "You're Fired." The Feeling is Great and the Extra Paychecks Earned for Firing Your Boss Feel Greater.

- Winning the Lottery? Begging for Raise? Waiting for an Inheritance? They're Rolled into One with Extra Paychecks Earned from Working Your Own Business.

- Pleading for Days Off? Begging for Extra Vacation Time from the Almighty Boss? It's Humiliating. Now, You Can Take Off Any Day You Choose Without the Humiliation of Pleading and Begging.

- Hate Working for a Vampire Blood-Sucking Boss? It Doesn't Seem Fair that You Get Two Weeks a Year for Yourself and Pay Two Weeks A Year for Your Boss.

- Putting Your Arms Around Your Work 50-Hours a Week? It's Not Like Putting Your Arms Around Your Spouse and Children After Working 15-Hours a Week. It's Time for Change.

- Marriage is Time spent for Kids, Spouse and Family. Make Time for Your Kids, Spouse, Family and Marriage. Make More Money Part-Time than You Make Full-Time so You Can Spend Time for Your Kids, Spouse and Family.

- Getting a 2% Raise Once a Year is a Big Deal. Getting a 7% Raise Once a Month is a Bigger Deal. The 2% Raise Once a Year Comes from Your Boss. The 7% Raise Once a Month Comes from Your Own Network Marketing Business.

- Hate Working 40-Years of Hard Labor and Retiring on 60% of What You Cannot Live On? Retire in 5-Years with Us at Full Pay.

- Feel Like Talking to Your Boss about a Raise is Like Banging Your Head against the Wall? Get a 7% Raise with Us Once a Month.

- Imagine if Your Bills Got Smaller and Your Bank Account Got Bigger. No, that Won't Happen with Your Job, but it Will Happen with Us.

- Who Makes More Money? You or the Boss? Who Has More Fun? You or the Boss? The Boss Has More Fun and Makes More Money. You Have Less Time to Have Money and Less Money to Enjoy It.

- Which is More Fun? Commuting in Traffic Coming and Going and Taking Away One Hour of Your Valuable Time? Or, To Come and Go from Your Bedroom to Your Computer and Make Extra Paychecks for Your Valuable Time?

- Parents Told You What to Do. Teachers Told You What to Do. Your Boss Tells You What to Do. Want to Turn It Around and Collect Bonus Checks for Life and Not Have Anyone Tell You What to Do?

- Like a Rock Star, Do Something Once and Get Paid Over and Over Again for Life. Write a Song Once and the Rockstar Gets Paid Royalties for Life. Sponsor Some People Once and Collect Money Over and Over Again for Life.

- There are Two Types of People in the World. Those Who Get Word-of-Mouth Advertising Bonus

Checks in their Bank Accounts Once a Month. And Those who don't. Which Group Would You Like to Be In?

Whew!! That's a lot. Now, it's your turn to make some great Word Pictures. Word Pictures are a skill to learn and will make you more money than stating facts.

Chapter 3:
The Profile Description.

Feel like your profile description on LinkedIn is a resume begging for a job? I once **felt** the same way. What I've **found** is if I change my profile to feature benefits for Network Marketers, I get better results.

Our profile description is a formula. Guess what it is? **Feel + Felt + Found**. I know how you **feel** about your problem. I once **felt** the same way. What I've **found** for fixing it is this.

Why does the formula work? Empathy! It empathizes with the reader.

People don't care for how you think. They care for how you feel. They care for what you've found for making them feel better.

Network Marketers are in the relationship business. Professional Network Marketers don't put dollar signs on people. We recognize people and people's problems. We feel for the people and their problems.

Feel + Felt + Found empathizes with the reader. The reader feels you care about his pain, his struggle, and his hurts. Real empathy is relieving the pain, removing the struggle and soothing the hurt.

We will flesh out the pieces for each part of our "**Feel + Felt + Found**" formula.

The number one rule for profile descriptions? Stay with your theme. Whatever theme you've started for your **backdrop slogan**, you'll keep in your description.

- If your backdrop slogan starts with a free car, your profile will talk about free cars.
- If your backdrop slogan is about health, your description is about health.
- If your backdrop slogan is about Network Marketing, your description is about Network Marketing.

Let's put together our formula for **Feel + Felt + Found** by adding bones, muscle and skin to flesh it out.

We're going to tell a story with three parts.

- Tell me about a problem you feel right now.
- I'll tell you how I felt about the problem.
- Then I'll show you what I've found for fixing the problem.

At the end of the story, we'll issue a call to action and provide a few links

(1). Feel.

We'll need a first sentence for introducing the problem that other people feel. A first sentence is a sentence that we'll make interesting for getting our prospect's attention. It states the problem without it reading like it's a tech manual.

Story One: Which first sentence is more interesting?

(**A**). Our business opportunity gives tax advantages that can reduce your overhead by 28% to 31%.

Or,

(**B**). Let me tell you about Jerry. Jerry is a single working dad who got behind on his taxes and was drowning in debt. Now, he earns an extra $500 a week that paid off his tax burden and bills. He spends more time at home with his children from the extra income he earns.

Story Two: Which first sentence is more interesting?

(**A**). Our weight loss product has 26 ingredients grown in the Amazonian Rain Forest and infused into an herbal all-natural tea.

Or,

(**B**). Let me tell you about Mary. Mary was 40 pounds overweight and in 30 days has lost 8 dress sizes by taking our Super Charged Weight Loss Teas.

Story Three: Which first sentence is more interesting?

(**A**). Our retirement plan can beat your retirement plan. We put the gross amount of money earned by the company into a general fund and distribute it. You're paid based upon the amount of money you have earned.

Or,

(**B**). Let me tell you about Jim. Jim worked for a vampire blood sucking boss that forced him to work 60-hour weeks of hard labor for ten years. He had no retirement plan. Now, after working five years with our business he fired his boss and retired at full pay.

For all three stories, story "**B**" is more interesting than story "**A**."

Notice the Formula for first sentences.

- Let Me Tell You About + A First Name.
- Problem 1 + (Problem 2 if You Choose) +
- Benefit 1 That Solves the Problem + (Benefit 2 If You Choose).

This is slicker than spit on a glass doorknob, right?

(2). Felt.

Let me tell you how I felt about this problem.

We are going to take our three stories with first sentences and build a profile.

Starting with story #1, list all the feelings and experiences that you have felt for Jerry's problems. List them 1, 2, 3 with as many feelings and experiences as you can think of. We may have to cull the herd later, but we want as much detail as we can get. I would list fifteen or more experiences and feelings.

Then list all your feelings for the second and third stories. Be creative but find some common ground.

The rule of thumb? Be brutally honest in your list about how you feel with the problem.

People love honesty. Being open and vulnerable makes you look smart and professional. It builds rapport and belief. Hiding things makes you look dishonest and unprofessional. It builds distrust and unbelief.

Ready for some examples?

- I was $10,000 in debt to the IRS.
- I was 50 pounds overweight.
- I had no retirement plan working for my company.
- The IRS put a lien on my property.
- I felt tired and run down all day.
- Social Security was not going to cut it for me.
- The IRS penalized me at a 5% tax rate per month.
- Little kids around the neighborhood called me fatty.
- My wife's retirement plan won't help us in the end.
- The IRS called my boss and my creditors.
- My weight problem prevented me from playing with my grandchildren.
- Because my bucket list was more expensive than my social security check, I had to empty the bucket.

You get the point. We'll need fifteen or more personal experiences and feelings about the problems in each story. This will assure our own stories have enough bone and flesh for building a profile.

(3). Found

Now, we are going to list benefits given by our offers

So far, we've listed problems. Now, we'll list benefits that our Network Marketing business offers for fixing the problems.

List no more than **three benefits** that your offers can give for solving the problems in each story. More than three benefits will confuse the reader. Three benefits are all we need for showing how to fix the problem. So, list only your **best benefits**.

Remember, we will list only benefits and not features.

- Pay raises each month for paying the IRS penalties.
- Products that melt 10 pounds in 8 days.
- Retirement in 5 years at full pay.
- Tax benefits of 28% to 32%.
- Products that burn belly fat and carbs.
- Vacations that fit the retirement budget.
- Tax attorney by the company to help people in need.
- Energy products to keep the body energized during activity.
- Guaranteed lifestyle bonus payments.

(4). The Call to Action

The call to action is a command. It commands prospects in a nice way to act.

Our first goal is to get the prospect's contact information. We'll achieve the goal by offering them a FREE product. In exchange, they will give us their contact information.

Our second goal is my favorite. We will make an offer for the prospects to book time with us for a telephone call. A link for your online calendar is the best method. This will become clearer as you read further.

Now, our profile begins to look like this.

Story One

Step #1: We'll use our first sentence for story #1.

Let me tell you about Jerry. Jerry is a single working dad who got behind on his taxes and was drowning in debt. Now, he earns an extra $500 a week that paid off his tax burden and bills. He spends more time at home with his children from the extra income he earns.

Step #2: List problems we have felt and experienced with Jerry.

- I was $10,000 in debt to the IRS.

- The IRS put a lien on my property.

- The IRS penalized me at a 5% penalty rate per month.

- The IRS called my boss and my creditors.

Step #3: List benefits we've found for fixing the problem.

- Pay raises each month for paying the IRS penalties.

- Tax benefits of 28% to 32%.

- Tax attorney by the company to help people in need.

Step #4: The Call to Action.

- All Home-Based Owners, Network Marketers and Entrepreneurs. I'd love to learn more about what's going on for you and your business. Book a Virtual Coffee Session so we can talk by telephone. Copy and paste the link: (**Link to your online calendar**).

Story Two

Step #1: We'll use our first sentence for story #2.

Let me tell you about Mary. Mary was 40 pounds overweight and in 30 days has lost 8 dress sizes by taking our Super Charged Weight Loss Teas.

Step #2: List problems we have felt and experienced with Mary.

- I was 50 pounds overweight.
- I felt tired and run down all day long.
- Little kids around the neighborhood called me fatty.
- My weight problem prevented me from playing with my grandchildren.

Step #3: List benefits we've found for fixing the problem.

- Products that melt 10 pounds in 8 days.
- Products that burn belly fat and carbs.
- Energy products to keep the body energized during activity.

Step #4: The Call to Action.

- All Home-Based Owners, Network Marketers and Entrepreneurs. I'd love to learn more about what's going on for you and your business. Book a Virtual Coffee Session so we can talk by telephone. Copy and paste the link: (**Link to your online calendar**).

Story Three

Step #1: We'll use our first sentence for story #3.

Let me tell you about Jim. Jim worked for a vampire blood sucking boss that forced him to work 60-hour weeks of hard labor for ten years. He had no retirement plan. Now, after working five years with our business he fired his boss and retired at full pay.

Step #2: List problems we have felt and experienced with Jim.

- I had no retirement plan working for my company.
- Social Security was not going to cut it for me.
- My wife's retirement plan won't help us in the end.
- Because my bucket list was more expensive than my social security check, I had to empty the bucket.

Step #3: List benefits we've found for fixing the problem.

- Retirement in 5 years at full pay.
- Vacations that fit the retirement budget
- Guaranteed lifestyle bonus payments.

Step #4: The Call to Action.

- All Home-Based Owners, Network Marketers and Entrepreneurs. I'd love to learn more about what's going on for you and your business. Book a Virtual Coffee Session so we can talk by telephone. Copy and paste the link: (**Link to your online calendar**).

See how easy it is to build a profile?

Now, we must flesh out our three stories with bones, muscles and skin in 2000 characters.

Story #1.

Let me tell you about Jerry. Jerry is a single working dad who got behind on his taxes and was drowning in debt. Now, he earns an extra $500 a week that paid off his tax burden and bills. He spends more time at home with his children from the extra income he earns.

So much of my life was like Jerry. I was dodging the IRS and fighting bill collectors. I changed my phone number several times. I closed the windows and blinds in my house. I dared not make any noise for fear of letting the tax collector know that I was home. None of it worked.

- I was $10,000 in debt to the IRS.

- The IRS put a lien on my property.

- The IRS penalized me at a 5% penalty rate per month.

- The IRS called my boss and my creditors.

- Because my bucket list was more expensive than my social security check, I had to empty the bucket.

Can you relate?

When I thought I was close to losing it all, a friend introduced me to Network Marketing. I never forget the night. Friday, December 5, 2016. That was the night everything changed for me.

I listened to a presentation and the presenter hit all my hot buttons. The way to remove the fear of the IRS. The way to beat the penalties. The way to finally be free from worry and stress.

I found how to get pay raises in days to pay off the IRS penalties of 5% a month. For the first time, I saw what owning my own business can do for me with the IRS… tax benefits of 28% to 32%.

And the *"crème de la creme?"* The company would help me by providing a tax attorney.

I know many of you have walked in Jerry and my shoes. We know the struggles. We know the successes.

Now, I want to help you. I want to help you create freedom from your job interfering with your week. I want to help you with the freedom to spend money without the fear of cost. I want to help you remove the shackles placed on your time.

And I want to help you dream dreams and turn dreams into reality.

All Home-Based Owners, Network Marketers and Entrepreneurs. I'd love to learn more about what's going on for you and your business. Book a Virtual Coffee Session so we can talk by telephone. Copy and paste the link: (**Link to your online calendar**).

Story #2.

Let me tell you about Mary. Mary was 40 pounds overweight and in 30 days has lost 8 dress sizes by taking our Super Charged Weight Loss Teas.

My weight has always been a problem for me. I seemed to gain it looking **at** food. Well, eating food didn't help too. No matter what I did, the weight would not come off. Exercise.

Eating funny tasting foods. Starving myself. None of these worked.

- I was 50 pounds overweight.

- I felt tired and run down all day long.

- Little kids around the neighborhood called me fatty.

- My weight problem prevented me from playing with my grandchildren.

Can you relate?

Then Mary came along. Mary showed me a cool organic all-natural weight loss tea. I was skeptical. I was leery. After all, I spent hundreds of dollars on weight loss programs. Fifty pounds overweight was all I got for my efforts.

Mary gave me a week sample of this amazing tea. I tried it for 8 days. Guess what? I lost 10 pounds. Wow!! I became sold. My waistline slimmed 2 inches.

Then Mary introduced me to another great product. An herbal coffee. Belly fat and all those empty carbs begin to burn away. My waistline dropped 10 inches in 30 days. Another product energized my body and turned it into a mean, lean fat burning machine. Little kids who once called me fatty now call me Sir. It's funny what losing weight can do for your self-esteem.

How many of you have been in my shoes? I'd love to book a session with you to talk.

There are two types of overweight people in the world. Those who want to do something about it. And those who don't. Which type are you?

All Home-Based Owners, Network Marketers and Entrepreneurs. I'd love to learn more about what's going on for you and your business. Book a Virtual Coffee Session so we can talk by telephone. Copy and paste the link: (**Link to your online calendar**).

Story #3.

Let me tell you about Jim. Jim worked for a vampire blood sucking boss that forced him to work 60-hour weeks of hard labor for ten years. He had no retirement plan. Now, after working five years with our business he fired his boss and retired at full pay.

Jim was miserable. His job kept him broke though he was making a six-figure income… there was more debt than income. He had no social life and no friends.

I don't know Jim, but I've known about him from stories in my company. I can relate to him. I had a vampire blood-sucking boss that made we work 50 to 60 hours a week and bring work home on the weekends.

- I had no retirement plan.
- Social Security was not going to cut it for me.
- My wife's retirement was less than $20,000 in a few mutual funds.

My bucket list? Forget it! I was emptying it faster than I could fill it. Things in my bucket were more expensive than what my Social Security could afford.

I was desperate to find something to bail me out from a sinking ship.

One night awakened by a restless night of worry and fret, I searched the internet. I found a person online in my hometown who helped people retire in 5-years at full pay. Wow!! That sounded too good to be true, but I decided to take the bait on the hook.

He showed me how I could retire in 5-years at full pay by following a 1,2,3 step by step system. First Class Vacations to Hawaii and Tahiti paid by the company was a dream come true.

Then I found out that the company pays lifestyle bonuses that affords you a new car and new home. Good! My old car and my old home were rough around the edges.

And the best part? I could work part-time on my fortune while working full-time at my job until I could fire my boss and walk away.

Six months later, I walked into my boss' office and looked him straight in the eye and said, 'YOU'RE FIRED!" He didn't appreciate it, but I didn't care how he felt. I walked away and never looked back.

All Home-Based Owners, Network Marketers and Entrepreneurs. I'd love to learn more about what's going on for you and your business. Book a Virtual Coffee Session so we can talk by telephone. Copy and paste the link: (**Link to your online calendar**).

Chapter 4:
Let's Finish Our Profile

(1). Links.

In the Profile Description form at the bottom, there are places for links. This is where you put something of value for the reader to click on. You want links for things of value that help solve problems for the reader.

- YouTube Videos.
- Blogs.
- Blog Articles.
- Websites.
- Funnels.
- Affiliate Programs.

The rule of thumb? DO NOT put any links for your company website.

What about selling stuff? Yes, put links for the things that you wish to sell. This includes links for your opportunity, products, services and affiliate programs.

Links for your company website are not a good idea. Links for videos on YouTube and articles for blogs are great ideas.

(2). Articles and Activities.

"Articles and Activities" are where you shine the most. "Articles and Activities" give you a chance for showing off your creativity.

The two things that go in "Articles and Activities"?

- Original articles.
- Original videos.

Original articles are articles written by you and published for LinkedIn. Original videos are videos created by you and uploaded for LinkedIn. Links for YouTube videos and articles found elsewhere are not acceptable.

Original articles should be no more than 500 words. People on LinkedIn don't have time for reading lengthy articles.

Original videos should never be more than 10-minutes. Two to five-minute videos work best. Any video beyond 9 minutes 59-seconds is unacceptable by LinkedIn and rejected.

For publishing original articles:

- Click the "Home Page" button.
- On Home Page is a "Start a Post" Button.
- Click "Write an Article" button.

For publishing original videos:

- Click the "Home Page" button.
- On Home Page is a "Start a Post" Button.
- Click the Video Icon to upload the video.

Give all videos a title and a one- or two-line summary statement. People do want to know what the video is all about.

I encourage you to use hashtags for both original articles and original videos.

What is the best content for publishing? Training material. Most Network Marketers like learning skills. Training material teaching skills works the best.

Where can you find content?

- Books.
- Articles.
- Blogs.
- Videos.
- Training webinars.
- Online and Offline magazines.
- Training programs.
- Audio files.

There are 25 skills to learn for Network Marketing. You can write and make videos on different ways for implementing these skills.

- Skill 1: The Secret Language of Prospects.
- Skill 2: How to Give A One Minute Presentation and Two Minute Stories.
- Skill 3: Ice Breakers – Prospecting for Appointments.

- Skill 4: Super Closing – The Decision-Making Part of The Brain.

- Skill 5: Needs vs Wants.

- Skill 6: Word Pictures.

- Skill 7: Understanding the Subconscious.

- Skill 8: How to Talk to The Subconscious.

- Skill 9: Commanding the Brain to Listen.

- Skill 10: Getting Prospects to Believe the Good Things You Say.

- Skill 11: Magic Sequence of Words.

- Skill 12: First Sentences and Headlines.

- Skill 13: Story Techniques to Bypass Negativity.

- Skill 14: Inclusive vs Exclusive Language.

- Skill 15: Creating Instant Rapport.

- Skill 16: Presentation and Public Speaking Mastery.

- Skill 17: Power Marketing and Headline Skills.

- Skill 18: How to Find Presold Prospects.

- Skill 19: Internet and Social Networking for Presold Leads.

- Skill 20: How-to Follow-up on Prospects.

- Skill 21: Creating Vision.

- Skill 22: Handling Problems.

- Skill 23: Locating (Prospecting).

- Skill 24: Teaching Leaders.

- Skill 25: Leadership Tests.

How do you create content?

- Step 1. Find a problem.
- Step 2: Offer solutions.
- Step 3. A call to actions.

Step #1: Introduce one and no more than two problems that people have.

- Jobs interfering with peoples' lives.
- Turning "no-decisions" into "yes-decisions."
- Bills getting bigger and bank accounts getting smaller.
- Salaries limiting what we can afford.

Step #2: Make a list of benefits from your Network Marketing offers for solving the problems.

- How to work part-time on your fortune while working full-time at your job.
- How to turn "no-decisions" into "yes-decisions."
- How to make bills smaller and bank accounts bigger.
- How to get a 7% pay raise a month.

Mentioning the name of your company, products and services is not advisable.

Step #3: Give a call to action.

- Click this.
- Try this.
- Look here.
- Read this.

- Listen to this audio.

- Watch this video.

- Go to my online calendar.

Take step #1, step #2 and step #3 and make your video or write your article. Create your material around a narrative, event, story, person, place... etc.

Want content for guiding you? **DaleMoreau.net** or **BigAlBooks.Com**.

The rule of thumb? Write one and no more than two articles a day and create one and no more than two videos a day.

I can hear the whining and gnashing of teeth... Dale, I can't do one or two articles and videos a day. You can learn. Use YouTube for a source. It has training videos for helping you create video content and articles.

Remember, our job on LinkedIn is to look smart and be professional. We are dealing with people on LinkedIn who are smart and professional. Nothing impresses them more than acting like a professional. Original content in articles and videos twice a day makes you look smart and be professional.

(3). Experience.

LinkedIn works best as a list for all our experiences and professional work with Network Marketing.

Four parts for the experience section matter the most.

- School.

- Activities and Societies.

- From Year and To Year

- Media.

We can ignore all the other parts.

(1). "School" is a required field. Here is where we will put your training classes for Network Marketing. Type "Network Marketing" and a drop-down menu appears. Ignore the drop-down menu. Instead, type something related to your Network Marketing training.

- Network Marketing Academy.
- School of Network Marketing.
- Rank Master Advanced.

(2). "Activities and Societies" are fields for describing our tools. if we put a video for explaining your experiences, you will need to describe the video. If we put a website, we'll need to describe what our website is about. Any program, video, article, audio file, etc., will need a brief description for what it's about.

(3). You must put a date for "From Year" and "To Year." Choose any date you want.

(4). "Media" is the place for links or uploads. A link for a video on YouTube or an upload for a video work well here.

Pretty simple, right?

Add several media types for the "Experience" section of your profile. I have six for myself.

(4). Education.

Education has four parts.

- Field of Study.

- Activities and Societies.
- From Year and To Year
- Media.

Ignore all the other parts.

"Education" is for training programs we've attended. Webinars, seminars, Network Marketing events, classes, training programs are acceptable here.

"Field of Study" is where you will type the name of the training program that you attended. Want some examples?

- Mastermind Event.
- MasterClass for Network Marketers.
- Rank Masters.
- "Activities and Societies" is the description of the program you attended.

You must put a date for "From Year" and "To Year." Choose the dates that you attended classes or webinars. If you don't know the dates, make a good estimate.

Media is the place for links and uploads. Videos, articles, audio, websites, affiliate programs, images, funnels, lead magnets will work.

Add two or three training programs for the "Education" section. Add more training programs if you have more.

(5). Volunteer Experience.

"Volunteer Experience" is the place for lots of benefits.

Seven sections matter for "Volunteer Experience."

- Organization.
- Role.
- Cause
- Start Date
- Check Mark by "**I Currently Volunteer Here.**"
- Description.
- Call to Action.

"Organization" should start with the phrase "**Helping People...**"

"Role" is for slogans representing your niche. Since there are so many slogans to choose from, I will only provide three examples.

Training Ordinary Persons to Become Extra-Ordinary Network Marketers.

- Like any Machine, the Body Runs Best When Operated According the Designs of Nutrition.
- Helping Others Achieve Their Goals of Financial Freedom in Record Time.

"Cause" is a drop-down menu. Choose the closest niche that represents your Network Marketing Business. For example, if you are in the health and wellness business, choose "HEALTH" from the drop-down menu. "Health" is the closest you'll find for "health and wellness."

"Start Date" can be anything you choose. It does not matter.

You must place a check mark by "**I Currently Volunteer Here**." Don't leave it off. Otherwise, you won't be seen by others.

"Description" is for lots of benefits. Our goods, services and opportunity are full of great benefits. Here is where we will share them.

Remember our formula "**I show people how to**" + "**a benefit**?" We are going to drop "I show people how to" and list only the benefits with three dashes in front of them.

- ...Get an extra paycheck twice a month.

- ...Work less time than our parents.

- ...Retire in 5-years at full pay.

- ...Buy a college instead of attending a college.

- ...Take one-week paid holidays once a month and not stay with our in-laws.

- ...Get healthy and get paid for it.

- ...Lose weight without going to the gym or eating funny tasting foods.

- ...Never have to go to work again.

- ...Take a five-day weekend with full pay instead of a two-day weekend with no pay.

- ...Live in five-star hotels at one-star rates while we travel.

- ...Wake up early every morning feeling like a million bucks.

- ...Fall asleep within five minutes of our heads touching the pillow.

Place eight to ten of your best benefits in the "Description" field. Be sure to double-space between each new line.

After you have all your benefits listed, put a call to action at the end of the description field.

Why did we drop the phrase "I show people how to" in front of the benefits? It's not necessary. Remember how we put "Helping People..." in the "organization" field? The phrase "helping people..." replaces the phrase "I show people how to..."

(6). Skills and Endorsements.

"Skills and Endorsements" are easy.

There are two rules.

- Get rid of all the skills that make your "Skills and Endorsement" section look like a resume for a job.
- Choose skills related to Network Marketing.

If you cannot find skills from the drop-down menu, type in some skills. Make sure you have those skills. Don't put skills that you cannot justify for yourself.

Here are some suggestions.

- Network Marketing.
- At Home Business.
- Home-Based Business.
- Work from Home.
- Work from Home Business.
- MLM.
- Multilevel Marketing.

- Multilevel Marketing Business.
- Blogging.
- Sales.
- YouTube.
- YouTube Marketing.
- Nutrition.
- Health and Wellness.
- Vlogging.
- Article Marketing.
- Article Writing.
- Videos.
- Video Marketing.
- Network Marketing Professional.
- Marketing Strategy.
- Social Media.
- Social Media Marketing.
- Entrepreneurship.
- Strategic Planning.
- Business.
- Small Business.
- Affiliate Marketing.
- Facebook.
- Facebook Marketing.
- Twitter.

- Twitter Marketing.
- Training.
- Coaching.

List at least 15 skills having to do with Network Marketing. LinkedIn has a system called "algorithms." Algorithms help rank you in the LinkedIn search engine and newsfeeds. So, the more skills you list, LinkedIn will rank you higher in its search engine and newsfeeds.

(7). Recommendations.

If you are brand new to LinkedIn, leave this section alone until later. You are not going to get many endorsements. No one knows you enough for you to get any endorsements.

Endorsements come from people who trust your skills. The more that people will come to know you for your expertise, the more endorsements you'll get. Endorsements come under the "Skills and Endorsement" section of your profile page.

Many established Network Marketers on LinkedIn have but only a few endorsements.

Many of you are long-time LinkedIn users, but you're starting out new in Network Marketing. So, you won't have many endorsements for Network Marketing. Don't worry, you'll get endorsements over time. I will show you later how to get endorsements. Be patient or read faster.

(8). Accomplishments.

If you have any Network Marketing credentials, here is where you will place them.

- Click the "+" button and a drop-down menu will appear.

- Choose "Publications," "Certifications," "Course" "Project" "Honor and Award" "Test Score," "Language" or "Organization."

- For every category you choose, you must provide a name. For example, if you were to choose 'Publications," you will provide the name for the publication. If you were to choose "Certificates," you will provide the name for the Certificate.

(9). Interests.

"Interests" pretty much takes care of itself when you join groups on LinkedIn. The more groups you will join, "Interests" will populate the groups.

Chapter 5:
What's Public and Private?

Settings are public and private. There are some things in the settings we'll want public. Other things in the settings we'll want private.

This section is very important. The right settings grant access for your connections to buy your products. The wrong settings won't let your connections see your profile.

To find Settings:

- Click on "**Me**" at the top of your LinkedIn page.

- A drop-down menu will appear.

- Click "Settings and Privacy."

- On the "**Settings and Privacy**" page, you'll find four tabs.

- Account tab.

- Privacy tab.

- Ads tab.

- Communications tab.

One by one we will go through the settings.

(1). Accounts Tab.

We will start with the "Account" tab. Click on it to open. There are five sections with several features.

- Section #1: Login and security.

- Section #2: Site preferences.

- Section #3: Subscriptions and payments.

- Section #4: Partners and services

- Section #5: Account management.

Follow the instructions with each section.

Section #1. Login and Security.

- *Email Address*: If you don't see your email address, this is the time for adding it. Or, you can remove old email addresses. Choose one primary email address if you have more than one.

- *Phone Number*: Add phone numbers. Delete phone numbers. Make sure you put a valid phone number.

- *Change Password*: Here you can change your password. If you do change it, be sure you have your old password handy. You'll need it to complete the transaction.

- *Where You're Currently Signed In*: Leave this alone. If you chose to sign out of all sessions showing, here you may do so.

- *Two-Step Verification*: Turn this feature to Off.

Section #2. Site Preferences.

- *Language*: Set the language that you speak.

- *Showing Profile Photos*: Click the drop-down menu and chose "**All LinkedIn Members**."

- *Feed Preferences*: Leave this alone.

- *Name, Location, and Industry*: Leave this one alone.

- **Section #3. Subscriptions and Payments**.

- *Manage Premium Account*: If you have purchased a subscription for a premium account, here is where you can manage it. If you have not purchased a premium account, ignore this.

- *View Purchase History*: Leave this part alone.

Section #4: Partners and Services.

- *Microsoft*: Ignore this service.

- *Permitted Services*: Here you can grant LinkedIn access to services such as your LinkedIn Account and Cell Phone. Allow LinkedIn access to both.

- *Twitter Settings*: Remember what I told you about Twitter in an earlier chapter? Well, here is where you will add your Twitter Account. If you have Twitter, add your account. If you don't have Twitter, ignore this setting.

Section #5: Account Management. Follow the instructions below for this section.

- *Merging LinkedIn Accounts*: You can merge several LinkedIn accounts into one. Otherwise, ignore this.

- *Closing Your LinkedIn Account*. Ignore this unless you want to waste the money you spent on this book. (I'm joking).

Easy, agreed?

(2). Privacy Tab

Click "Privacy" to open. There are five sections with several features.

- Section #1: How others see your profile and network information.

- Section #2: How others see your LinkedIn activity.

- Section #3: How LinkedIn uses your data.

- Section #4: Job seeking preferences.

- Section #5: Blocking and hiding.

Follow the instructions for each section.

Section #1: How Others See Your Profile and Network Connections.

- *Edit Your Public Profile.* Click on "Edit Your Public Profile." Your profile page appears.

- Turn "**Your Profile's Public Visibility**" to ON.

- Turn "**Name, Number of Connections, Industry, and Region**" to ON.

- Turn **"Public"** to ON.

- Turn all 15 buttons under "**Public**" to ON.

Refresh the page and when you see your public "mug shot" appear, you'll know the settings are working. If you do not see your "mug" under 'Public Profile Settings," wait a few minutes and refresh the page. Now, it should appear.

Now, navigate back to the "Settings and Privacy" page and click on "Privacy." Are you back? Great!

- *Who Can See Your Email Address?* Click the drop-down menu and choose **Anyone on LinkedIn**.

- *Who Can See Your Connections?* Click the drop-down menu and choose **Only You**.

- *Viewers of this Profile Also Viewed*. Turn this feature to NO.

- *Who Can See Your Last Name?* Choose your profile listed. If more than one exists, choose one only.

- *Representing Your Organization and Interests*: Turn this feature to YES.

- *Profile Visibility Off LinkedIn*: Turn this feature to YES.

- *Microsoft Word.* Turn this feature to YES.

Section #2: How Others See Your LinkedIn Activity.

- *Profile Viewing Options*: Chose the profile you wish for others to see.

- *Manage Active Status*: Check mark **All LinkedIn Members**.

- *Sharing Profile Edits*: Turn this feature to NO.

- *Notifying Connections When You're in the News*: Turn this feature to YES.

- *Mentions or Tags by Others*: Turn this feature to YES.

Section #3: How LinkedIn Uses Your Data.

- *Manage Your Data and Activity*: Ignore this feature.

- ***Download Your Data***: You can download your LinkedIn data here. Otherwise, ignore this feature.

- ***Manage Who Can Discover Your Profile from Your Email Address***: Click the drop-down menu and choose EVERYONE.

- ***Manage Who Can Discover Your Profile from Your Phone Number***: Click the drop-down menu and choose EVERYONE.

- ***Sync Contacts***: Here you can sync contacts with your Google Calendar. Otherwise, ignore this feature.

- ***Sync Calendar***: Sync Google Calendar with LinkedIn. Otherwise, ignore this feature.

- ***Salary Data on LinkedIn***: Ignore this feature.

- ***Clear Search History***: Here is where you can clear all your search history. Ignore this feature. You will want to maintain your search history.

- ***Personal Demographic Information***: Ignore this feature.

- ***Social, Economic and Workplace Research***: Turn this feature to YES.

Section #4: Job Seeking Preferences.

- ***Job Application Settings***: Ignore this feature.

- ***Let Recruiters Know You're Open to Opportunities***: Turn this feature to NO. You are not seeking for a job with your profile. We create your profile strictly for Network Marketing.

- ***Signal Your Interest to Recruiters at Companies You Have Created Job Alerts For***: Turn this feature to "No."

- ***Sharing Your Profile when You Click Apply***: Turn this feature to NO.

- ***Stored Job Applicant Accounts***: Ignore this feature.

Section #5: Blocking and Hiding:

- ***Followers***: Click the drop-down menu and choose EVERYONE ON LINKEDIN. Turn the feature to NO for "Make Follow Primary."

- ***Blocking***: Here is where you can find a list of people whom you've blocked. Otherwise, ignore this feature.

- ***Unfollowed***: Here you can see who you have unfollowed. Otherwise, ignore this feature.

(3). Ads Tab.

Click "Ads" to open. There are three sections with several features.

- General Advertising Preferences.

- Data Collected on LinkedIn.

- Third Party Data.

Section #1: General Advertising Preferences.

- ***Insights on Websites You Visited***: Turn this feature to YES.

- ***Ads Beyond LinkedIn***: Turn this feature to YES.

- **_Profile Data for Ad Personalization_**: Turn this feature to YES.

Section #2: Data Collected on LinkedIn.

- **_Interest Categories_**: Turn this feature to YES.

- **_Connections_**: Turn this feature to YES.

- **_Locations_**: Turn this feature to YES.

- **_Demographics_**: Turn this feature to YES.

- **_Companies for You_**: Turn this feature to YES.

- **_Groups_**: Turn this feature to YES.

- **_Education_**: Check mark all features listed.

- **Job Information**: Features shown to related to Network Marketing need to a check mark. For features not related, you can uncheck them.

- **_Employer_**: Check mark all features related to Network Marketing. If the features are not related to Network Marketing, uncheck the features.

Section #3: Third Party Data.

- **_Interactions with Businesses_**: Turn BOTH features to YES.

- **_Ad-Related Actions_**: Turn this feature to YES.

(4). Communications Tab.

Click "Communications" to open. There are four sections with several features.

- Channels.

- Preferences.
- Groups.
- LinkedIn Messages.

Section #1: Channels.

- ***Notifications on LinkedIn***: Ignore this feature
- ***Email Frequency***: Check mark ALL features.

Section #2: Preferences.

- ***Who Can Send Your Invitations?*** Check mark **"Everyone on LinkedIn."**
- ***Messages from Members and Partners***: Turn ALL THREE features to YES.
- ***Read Receipts and Typing Indicators***: Turn this feature to YES.
- ***Message Reply Suggestions***: Turn this feature to YES.

Section #3: Groups.

- ***Group Invitations***: Turn this feature to YES.

Section #4: LinkedIn Messages.

- ***Participate in Research***: Turn this feature to YES.

Pat yourself on the back and take a few bows before a mirror. All the housekeeping is out of the way. Now, it's time to get to the good stuff.

Chapter 6:
Let's Get Mental.

There's an old saying that social media marketing is more about psychology than technology. Social media psychology is about getting people on our side. It's about getting people to make "yes-decisions."

Network Marketing's purpose for us is to get "yes-decisions." For every "yes-decision" we get, we make money. For every "no-decision" we get, we make zero money. We must get our prospects to buy our products and join our team.

We must know what makes people say "yes" and "no." If we are going to reach Network Marketers on LinkedIn, we need to understand how they think.

Brain science has helped us to unravel the mystery for how people make yes-decisions. The logical part of our brains is the conscious mind. The emotional part of our brains is the subconscious mind.

The subconscious mind makes all our decisions. Decisions are never made in the conscious mind. The subconscious mind tells the conscious mind how to think. It tells the conscious mind what to do.

Larry is an ordinary guy. He's not thinking about starting an opportunity. We meet Larry and come off like a salesperson. Larry's sales resistance radar goes up.

Why?

Sometime in the past, Larry's mom warned him about salespeople. Her warnings were constant. She instilled into him about how salespeople are sleazy. She harped on how salespeople trap you with complex contracts.

Then we come along. We come off like a salesperson. The internal program in Larry's subconscious mind raises a red flag. Larry says "no" to our offers.

The conscious mind is the size of a pea and can make only one decision at a time. It understands facts, figures, math, statistics, and anything in a logical linear order. It can't keep two thoughts in a person's head at the same time.

The subconscious mind is the size of a sixteen-story building. It can make millions of decisions at one time. It has internal programs telling us what to do.

- Watch out for that Network Marketing guy.

- Network Marketing is a pyramid.

- I don't like selling.

- I don't have the money.

- I don't have the time.

The subconscious mind controls the rational logical mind. Values, wants, benefits, and needs all come from the subconscious mind. People are value-pursuing beings before they are rational beings. What a person loves will be what a person will pursue. And that person will use any logical means for justifying their method for obtaining it.

If we appeal to prospects by spouting off facts, figures and features, we'll fail. If we appeal to prospects by talking values, wants, needs and benefits, we'll succeed.

So, we come along and meet a new prospect. We talk to him about:

- The 1,600 ingredients in our products.
- How our scientists can beat up your scientists.
- How our opportunity will make us millions.

What decision do think the prospects will make? No!!

But if we come along and appeal to the new prospect's subconscious mind with:

- Retiring in 5-years at full pay,
- Making more money part-time than he makes full-time,
- Taking two-week holidays and getting paid for four.

What decision do you think the prospects will make? Yes!!

Five triggers must happen in sequence before prospects will make "yes-decisions." Get any one trigger out of sequence and our prospects will not buy or join. Keep all five triggers in sequence and we will have instant success.

We owe Tom "Big Al" Schreiter a big round of applause for giving us the five triggers.

- Who are you?
- Can I trust and believe you?
- Are you interesting?

- Do I want to or not?

- Can you give me the details?

(1). Who Are You?

Prospects make harsh judgements. It is part of the internal programming in their subconscious minds. It keeps them safe and from harm.

A prospect meets an expert in his field. The prospect then meets a person who is not an expert in any field. Who would the prospect trust more?

A prospect meets a movie star on the street. The movie star is someone he idolizes. A prospect meets a stranger on the street for first time. Who would the prospect respect more?

The answer is obvious. The expert and movie star will win.

So, we're brand new to Network Marketing. We are not an expert. We are not a movie star. How can we impress the prospect?

There is no easy way for saying it. The new Network Marketer better become the expert and the star. We call this personal development.

Personal development is not about having a great attitude. Attitude alone will not get the prospects on our side.

Personal development will get us 75% of the way. Skills will get us the other 25%. The fact you have bought this book, you have shown your attitude is 75%. The other 25% is learning skills.

Personal development is about becoming the expert by the skills we learn. The more skills we can learn, the more positive our attitude will become.

When we are new to Network Marketing, we bring all our skills from our job into Network Marketing.

Would a carpenter's skills make him an expert in brain surgery? Would a brain surgeon's skills make him a good carpenter? The skills we know as a carpenter or a doctor do not make us an expert in Network Marketing. We must learn a new set of skills.

There are 25-skills to learn for Network Marketing. An earlier chapter lists them. Part of being an expert is the professionalism we will show in our profile. Make our profile on LinkedIn look smart and be professional and we will become the expert in the eyes of others.

The other part is the content we give away with our articles and videos. Give away great content and it makes you the expert even more.

Take 15-minutes out of each day to learn the skills for being the expert. We can all take 15-minutes out of our day for learning some new skills.

Listen to an audio file. Read a few pages of a book that teach one of the 25-skills in Network Marketing. Watch a video online. YouTube is full of short training videos for teaching the skills for Network Marketing. Webinars are a great way for learning the skills. Read a blog. "**DaleMoreau. Net**" has articles and videos for teaching people the skills for Network Marketing.

If you don't learn the skills for Network Marketing, you will not reach Network Marketers on LinkedIn.

Many Network Marketers on LinkedIn lack the skills. It's unfortunate but true. Many have never reached success. Most have made less than $100. They've never taken the time to learn new skills, or they were never taught the skills. They operate on their job skills and not on their Network Marketing skills.

So, we come along. We have the skills. We are the expert. How will prospects on LinkedIn react? They'll flock to us in great numbers.

Learning the right skills means taking on great responsibility. The prospect who joins our team will need training. We must take time out for teaching him the skills. But if we don't know the skills, we can't teach the skills.

Let's learn the skills so we and our team members are not left groping in the dark.

Five core skills taught in a short period of time will be enough to get a new Network Marketer going on his own.

The five core skills?

- Building rapport.
- Breaking the ice.
- Closing.
- Handling objections.
- Giving presentations.

Skill #1: Building rapport is knowing how to get people to like, trust and believe us.

Skill #2: Breaking the ice is knowing how to introduce our offers into a social conversation.

Skill #3: Closing is knowing how to get people across the finish line.

Skill #4: Handling objections is knowing how to turn no-decisions into yes-decisions.

Skill #5: Giving presentations is knowing how to get our message inside the prospects' heads.

We'll learn these skills in the next few chapters.

(2). Can I Trust You and Believe You?

Prospects are skeptical by nature. Internal programs inside the subconscious mind are telling them, "Let the buyer beware." They learned it from an earlier age. Momma and papa had warned them about strangers bearing gifts of shiny objects. These internal programs protect the prospects.

Protection is a good trait to have. It protects people from the bad guys. But it also over-protects them from the good guys. "Over-protection" will lump anybody who sells things into the "sleazy salesperson" category.

How can we beat the "over-protection racket?" If the prospects don't trust us, then they won't like us. They won't believe anything we say.

We have seven seconds with the prospects for building trust, belief and likability. Go beyond the seven seconds and we've lost them.

It's not fair, but we must deal with the hand dealt to us. Amateurs waste the first seven seconds. Professionals know how to manage the first seven seconds.

No matter where we meet them, we have only seven seconds to get the prospects to like us, trust us and believe us. On the streets or at church or online, it does not matter. Seven seconds are all we have.

The prospect lands on our LinkedIn profile page. He will spend seven-seconds on our page for his subconscious mind to determine if it is worth his time. If he likes what he sees, he will stay. If he doesn't like what he sees, he will move on.

So, we connect with a prospect through LinkedIn messenger. We have seven seconds to build instant trust, likability and belief. So, we better make it count.

(3). Are You Interesting?

We have lots of competition on social media. Twitter, Facebook, Snapchat and LinkedIn all have people competing for our attention.

Television, radio, magazines, and podcasts send us thousands of bits of data every day. They beg us every day to give them our eyes and ears.

If we want our voice heard, we must rise above the competition. We must outthink the competition. We must outsmart the competition. We must outcompete the competition.

We must be a cut above the best.

Coca Cola, Amazon and Apple are the big boys we must compete against every day. We don't have the budget or the time to beat them.

Vying for people's attention is hard when you're competing against other Network Marketers. It's our words against their words. The one with better words will win.

Amateur Network Marketers waste time with words that don't work. Professionals manage the words that do work. We have ten seconds for making our words interesting after building trust. So, we better make our words more interesting than our competition.

We meet Joseph on LinkedIn. Joseph listened to one other presentation before meeting us. The other presentation was perfect. So, we come along. We give a perfect presentation.

Joseph is thinking, "What makes your stuff better than the other guy's stuff?" Our compensation plan is the same as the other guy's compensation plan. Our products are the same as the other guy's products. Our presentation is the same as the other guy's presentation.

Joseph makes the decision to go with the other guy. Why? Better words that were more interesting. Our competition spoke better words more interesting than our words.

Speak words that are better and more interesting. If they are not interesting for the prospect, then it's goodbye forever.

Most prospects already want what we offer. They are presold on wanting healthier happier lives. They are presold on discount travel. They are presold on an extra paycheck. They are presold on lower utility bills.

It is how we present our offers to the prospects that make the difference. Our job is to convince them by using the right words. Too many times we talk them out of joining our team or buying our products by using the wrong words.

Want the eyes and ears of our prospects only on us? We better know how to make our stuff more interesting than our competition's stuff.

(4). Do I Want to or Not?

Closing is finding out if the prospects want what we have or not. Most amateur Network Marketers think closing happens at the end of the presentation. Professionals know it happens before the presentation.

Kelly determines our words are interesting. Now Kelly must decide if she wants what we offer or not. Kelly will make her decision in fifteen seconds. If we can dig our way through the first fifteen seconds, we are home free. Kelly will make a "yes-decision."

Prospects fear making decisions. Wrong decisions for them mean derision and rejection by family and friends. Right decisions mean they fear that meeting the challenge will be difficult. Our job is to help prospects overcome their fear of uncertainty and change.

Here is the reality. We invite the prospects to look at our offers. Immediately, the programs in their subconscious minds kick into high gear. They remember the last time they received a similar invitation. They accepted the invitation. They went online and ended up spending $20.00 for a registration fee to a webinar. And the webinar was three hours long. It wasted time and money for the prospect. Time they could have spent watching Monday night football. And money better spent buying pizza.

Closing prepares the prospect to accept change and uncertainty without fear. It prepares the prospects to think, "Yes, I want what you offer." We want them to turn off the salesman alarms. We want them to not resist change. We want them to believe the good things about our offers. We want them to listen. Closing will open the mind, and an open-minded prospect will listen.

(5). Can You Give Me the Details?

So, you've met a new prospect and here's what you've done in sequence.

- Spent 15-minutes a day to learn new skills.
- Spent 7-seconds with the prospect building trust, likability and belief.
- Spent 10-seconds with the prospect making your offer interesting.
- Spent 15-seconds on the prospect to determine if he or she wanted what you had to offer or not.

What about the time it takes to spend on the fifth trigger, "Can you give me the details?" Manage the first four triggers in sequence, then you'll have all the time you need.

We don't want to take advantage of our prospect's generosity. Their time is valuable. Make your presentation no more than two-minutes and you'll impress the prospect. An upcoming chapter will show you how.

Prospects make yes-decisions way early before the presentation. We want to only give presentations to prospects who ask for them. Too many times amateur Network Marketers do the opposite. They give presentations to people who never ask for them.

Professionals know "yes-decisions" happen early in the game. Presentations are only given to prospects who beg them for one. They know how to use words for getting prospects pleading for a presentation early in the game.

I can hear the skeptics now. How can we keep the five triggers in sequence? Stay tuned! Chapters that are coming up have your answer.

Chapter 7:
Building Rapport

We've been busy. Working on LinkedIn can exhaust us. The kinks and details behind the scenes with our profile and settings are tedious tasks. They are necessary if we wish to look smart and be professional.

Now, we need some "Me Time" that will make us money. We need to step back, take a time out and learn some new skills.

Network Marketing is in the business of getting yes-decisions. We don't get paid for getting no-decisions. We get paid for getting yes-decisions.

The path to getting yes-decisions is skills. Without skills, we will get no-decisions and be broke. With skills, we will get yes-decisions and be rich.

When we start out in Network Marketing, we have no skills. We have clerk skills. We have lawyer skills. We have baker skills. We have doctor skills. But we don't have Network Marketing skills.

So, we bring our job skills into Network Marketing. Job skills and Network Marketing skills do not mix well. They're like mixing oil and water. One races to the top. The other sinks to the bottom.

If we are going to be successful with Network Marketing, we must learn a new set of skills. There are 25-skills for Network Marketing to learn. Refer to an earlier chapter. You must take time out for yourselves and invest the time for learning these 25-new skills.

But today, we'll concentrate on only five skills.

- Building rapport.

- Breaking the ice.

- Closing.

- Handling objections.

- Presentations.

These five skills are the core for making Network Marketing work. They are the core for making LinkedIn work in your favor.

Let's unpack each skill. Here we'll start with building rapport. Other chapters to follow are dedicated to the other four skills.

Building rapport is the most important skill. Without mastering this skill, nothing that follows will work. No matter how good our opportunity may be, no one will believe us if we don't build rapport first.

Jack in is in the same Network Marketing company as Jill. They both have the same compensation plan. They both have the same products. They both have the same opportunity. They both have the same message.

Jill sells more products and signs up more team members than Jack.

Why? Rapport.

Jill builds a little bit of rapport before she begins to talk about her offers. Jack doesn't. Jack jumps head first into the conversation without building rapport and everybody scatters.

Rapport's purpose is to build relationships. Rapport's message is agreement. We build relationships by finding common ground with people. People like other people who are like them. They like people who see the world like they see it. They like people who agree with them.

- Do you feel comfortable at a church that does not have the same beliefs as yourself?
- Do you feel comfortable at political rallies that don't have your political views?
- Do you feel comfortable going to bars and meeting strangers who don't like what you like?

No! Of course not! You'll find it more comfortable being with people who like the same interests as yourself.

Prospects like people who are like them.

- They like people who speak the same language like them.
- They like people who eat the same foods like them.
- They like people who smile like them.

Would it not be in our best interest and the interest of the prospects to be like them?

Of course, it would.

Building rapport for amateur Network Marketers is like working with an erector set. There are lots of nuts and bolts and lots of headaches putting it together.

Amateur Network Marketers think honesty, integrity and sincerity builds rapport. These are great traits to have. But they do not build rapport.

Amateurs think F. O. R. M. will build rapport. F. O. R. M. is the acronym for "Family," "Occupation," "Recreation" and "Motivation." F. O. R. M. does not work for building rapport.

Building rapport for professionals is like playdough. It is pliable, easy to bend, and there are no hassles with the cleanup. Professionals build rapport by agreement. They are honest, truthful and sincere to facts that are agreeable with the prospects. They talk about family, occupation and motivation only **after** building rapport.

So, how do we build rapport? We will give the prospect a fact he already believes to be true.

Giving prospects facts that they believe true will make the prospects trust us, believe us, and like us. We will build instant rapport.

We give Sarah a fact that is true. What is going through Sarah's head?

"You gave me a fact that is true. You must think like me. You see the world like me. Because you think like me and see the world like I do, I can believe the things you'll tell me next."

Rapport is finding facts that people believe in and agree with.

Examples?

- Two paychecks are better than one.
- Pain comes with growing old.
- Wholesale is better than retail.
- Jobs interfere with our week.
- Our face is our first impression.

The prospect can agree with these facts. The facts are true for most people in life. The facts are reasonable for most people in life. The facts are believable for most people in life. Facts which are true, reasonable and believable will build rapport for most people.

Tell something that the prospect disagrees with and you won't build rapport.

Certain words added to facts will trigger programs that are deep-seated in our minds. These internal programs command us to make instant decisions.

You're a Democrat, and your neighbor is a Republican. You say, "Donald Trump" to your neighbor. Your neighbor most likely will smile and nod his head in agreement. You say "Barack Obama" to your neighbor, and he might not speak to you for a week.

Deep seated in our minds are millions of other programs that make decisions for us.

Walk into an office with people waiting for an appointment and smile. People will smile back. Sneeze in the same room and wait for the reactions. Certain people will sneeze.

Internal programs running in our minds trigger these reactions. They are telling us to do this and do that when certain events and words activate them.

One internal program stands out. Survival. We will survive at all cost.

People survive best when they are with groups. They feel safe and secure when they are with a crowd of people in strange places or a dark alley. No one wants to feel out of their comfort zone in a strange land or walk down a dark alley by themselves. Being with a group in a strange land makes them feel safe. Walking through a dark alley with a crowd makes them feel secure.

Think about the word phrases that represent groups.

- "Most people."
- "Everybody says."
- "Everybody knows."

When I say, "most people," the internal survival program takes over. It directs the conscious mind to react.

"I belong to most people. I am not part of 'less people.' I belong to a group of most people. And most people make me feel safe. So, I am going to stay with the 'most people' group. Since most people are what keeps me safe, I am going to believe what most people say."

I've built instant rapport.

Let's see how this works for Network Marketing.

- Most people want two paychecks.
- Most people prefer wholesale to retail.

- Most people want to retire early.
- Most people think jobs interfere with their lives.

Now, let's try some other examples.

- Everybody knows you get the extended warranty.
- Everybody knows our body comes with a lifetime guarantee.
- Everybody knows you can't get rich working a job.
- Everybody says it would be great to be rich.
- Everybody says working for someone else won't make us rich.
- Every mom says she want to protect their children from the other sick kids at school.

The formula?

- "Most People + A Problem" or "A Benefit."
- "Everybody Knows + A Problem" or "A Benefit."
- "Everybody Says + A Problem" or "A Benefit."

Now you can try it. List problems that most people and everybody have. List problems that your goods, services and opportunity can solve.

- Jobs.
- Money.
- Vacations.
- Wrinkles.
- Diets.
- Bills.

- Poverty.
- Taxes.
- Savings.
- Income.

Now, let's add one of our survival word phrases to these problems.

- Most people know jobs interfere with our lives.
- Everybody says they'd like more money.
- Everybody knows our wages limit the vacations we can afford.
- Most people want their skin looking younger.
- Everybody says dieting is an inconvenience.
- Everybody knows bills eat into our pay.
- Everybody says taxes are going higher.
- Most people want their bills decreased and their bank accounts increased.
- Everybody knows you can't get rich working on a limited income.

The best thing since apple pie, right?

Most people agree we've stated facts that are believable. Everybody knows our facts are true. Everybody says our facts are trustworthy. We've built instant rapport.

Other word phrases help us for building rapport.

- "If you're like me."
- "There's an old saying."

- "Well, you know how."

List some problems that your offers can solve.

- Passion.
- Antioxidants.
- Weekends.
- Work.
- Face.
- Retirement.
- Immunity.
- Commuting.
- Jobs.
- Wrinkles.
- Paychecks.
- Diets.

Add one of our magic phrases to the problem, and we will have instant rapport.

- If you're like me, you'll want fire in your belly for passion day and night.
- If you are like me, you'll want to protect your skin against the sun without that oily feeling.
- If you are like me, you'll want your weekends free.
- There's an old saying that work and no play makes Jack a dull boy.
- There's an old saying that our face is our first impression.

- There's an old saying that retirement is 45 years hard labor with a 60% cut in pay.
- Well, you know how our children are not immune from virus and germs at school?
- Well, you know how commuting takes one hour of our time each way?
- Well, you know how jobs guarantee that we'll be broke?
- Why do these three magic phrases work?

"**If you're like me**," triggers the emotional appeal to be someone else.

"I don't like being me. Sometimes, I'd rather be someone else. And because you said, 'If you're like me," I can be like you and make myself feel better."

Crazy, right? But it works.

"**There's an old saying**," triggers internal programs in the prospects' minds. It says,

"Old sayings have been around for a long time. If they've been around for a long time, old sayings must be believable and true. Otherwise, they would not be around for long. Since you said something that's been around for a long time, then I can believe what comes next."

"**Well, you know how**" triggers our curiosity bug.

"Well, you may know how, but I don't. And because you said, 'Well, you know how,' I must find out what you know that I don't. Otherwise I won't survive."

Can we use more than one rapport-building fact in a statement? Yeppers!

Combinations of rapport-builders will put building rapport on steroids.

- Most people know jobs interfere with our lives. There's an old saying that we are prisoners to a job that limits our time for family and play. Everybody knows we will work 40 years of hard labor with a 60% cut in pay. What kind of life is that?

- Well, you know how we want to protect our face from the sun while at the beach? There's an old saying that our face is our first impression. Most people who use this herbal tea for protecting the skin end up with a tan at the beach without the burn.

- Everybody knows bills eat into our pay. Most people want their bills lower and their bank accounts bigger. There's an old saying that jobs keep us broke. Don't you think we ought to do something about it?

- Everybody says they'd like more money. Everybody knows we'd have to work 50 to 60 hours a week or get a second job to make extra money. And well, you know how our jobs keep us broke? I just found out how to get a 7% raise a month without telling the boss. If you would ever like to know how, I'd be glad to show you. Meanwhile, what's for lunch?

- If you're like me, you want fire in your belly for passion day and night. Well, you know how age robs us of desire? Most people try this new berry juice to give them more energy during work or play.

Rapport! It's instant. It's fun, and it works when you know the secret for building it.

Chapter 8:
Breaking the Ice

How do we introduce our business into a social conversation?

Ice-breakers!

Once we've built rapport, it's easy to break the ice and introduce our offers into a social conversation. Ice-breakers don't work without building rapport.

(1). What Do You Do for a Living?

What is the number one question asked by most members on LinkedIn?

"What do you do for a living?" Or, **"what do you do?"**

LinkedIn is the perfect place for asking the question. LinkedIn is the perfect place for answering the question. LinkedIn is ready made for people who want to know "what do you do." It's listed in your profile, but they want to know the details.

"What do you do" is great for us. It gives us the first opportune moment for introducing our offers into a conversation.

Remember how we talked about making something interesting for grabbing people's attention? We'll want to grab people's attention by answering, "What do you do for a living?"

Here's the formula. **"I Show People How to" + A Benefit.**

List all the benefits that your goods, services and opportunity can offer. Make sure the benefits help for solving peoples' problems.

- Holidays.
- Weekends.
- Jobs.
- Pay.
- Raises.
- Bosses.
- College.
- Energy.
- Age.
- Hormones.
- Joints.
- Electricity.
- Non-Toxins.

Now, let's flesh out the benefits with our formula.

- I show people how to take 6-month holidays at full pay.
- I show people how to work two-days a week and get paid for five.

- I show people how to work part-time on their fortunes at full pay.
- I show people how to get a 7% pay raise every month without begging the boss.
- I show people how to fire their boss and walk away with full pay.
- I show people how to buy a college instead of attending a college.
- I show people how to give themselves more energy during work or play.
- I show people how to look 16-years younger all over again but with better judgment.
- I show people how to tune up their hormones for a well-balanced life.
- I show people how to give themselves the flexible joints of a 16-year old.
- I show people how to make their electricity bills smaller and bank accounts bigger.
- I show people how to clean their homes without polluting the environment.
- I show people how to clean their homes toxin and chemical free.

Now, you can try it! When people on LinkedIn ask you, "What do you do for a living?" you should have an answer. List all the benefits for your products, opportunity and services. Add the magic phrase "I show people how to…" and you'll answer the question.

"Dale, what do you do for a living?" "I show Network Marketers how to get more 'yes-decisions' from prospects than 'no-decisions'.

What happens if no one asks you, "What do you do for a living?" Then you'll ask them, "**What do you do for a living?**" After answering, the natural tendency for the prospect is to ask you, "So, what do you do for a living?"

- I show people how to tip the scales in their favor against acid stomach and sour breath.

- I show people a berry juice for keeping their urinary tracts in mint condition.

- I show people how to parch the thirst of their dried-out cells after an exhausting workout.

- I show people how to have more money for their health.

- I show people how to make big money for getting healthy.

- I show working moms how to stay home with their babies at full pay.

- I show millennials how to make more money part-time than their parents make full-time.

- I show secretaries how to make more money part-time than their boss makes full-time.

- I show people how to take five-star vacations at discount prices.

- I show sales people how to make more money part-time with wholesale than they make full-time with retail.

(2). You Must be a Natural.

Jill asked Bill on LinkedIn, "What do you do for a living?"

Bill said, "**I'm a computer technician**," but the prospect does not ask Jill, "What do you do?" So, Jill can't show her remarkable ice-breaker skills for what she does for a living.

What does Jill do? **"You Must Be a Natural." + "A Benefit of What the Prospects' Do."**

- "I'm in USANA." "You must be a natural at promoting and recommending your products online and off."

- "I am in Amway." "You must be a natural at promoting and recommending your opportunity on LinkedIn."

- "I am a hairstylist." "You must be a natural at doing your job."

- "I'm a life coach." "You must be a natural at helping people do what they cannot do for themselves."

- "I'm in an affiliate program." You must be a natural with products that support Network Marketing success."

- "I'm in weight management." "You must be a natural at helping people lose weight."

- "I'm in skincare." "You must be a natural at helping young people clear up their acne."

- "I'm a financial planner." "You must be a natural at helping people retire early."

- "I'm in Network Marketing." "You must be a natural at helping people fire their boss."

- "I'm in discounted utilities." "You must be a natural at helping peoples' utility bills get smaller and bank accounts get bigger."

- "I'm in travel." "You must be a natural at helping people travel at discount rates."

- "I'm in real estate." "You must be a natural at matching property owners with property buyers."

- "I'm in insurance." You must be a natural at helping people with peace of mind."

- "I'm in Information Technology." "You must be a natural at it."

If you don't know what benefits to add for "You must be a natural," you can say, **"You must be a natural at it."**

Why does "You Must Be a Natural" work? Three reasons!

- It is a recognition of their worth. It means someone is paying attention to me." It strokes their egos. We want to lift people up and compliment them for the things they do.

- It helps for building rapport. You are agreeing with something they do. They believe in what they do. They know what they do is true. They know what they do is reasonable, or they would not be doing it. Something that is true, reasonable and believable will build rapport.

- It provokes confession. Things might not be going well with the prospects. Their jobs may suck. Their

Network Marketing business may suck. Saying "you're a natural" contradicts the idea that things are going well. People will let you know that their jobs suck and their business sucks. They will let you know what problems they may have for solving.

Jill meets Mark on LinkedIn messenger. Jill tells Mark, "You must be a natural at promoting and recommending products online and off." Mark confesses, "Things are not going peachy as planned."

What's will be Jill's next response?" **"Would you like to do something about it?**

(3). I'm Just Curious Plus Tiny Questions.

Other magic phrases break the ice. **"I'm Just Curious"** + **"Tiny Questions"** + **"A Problem or A Benefit."**

"I'm just curious" works because it creates the desire for us to know things. Internal programs in our minds want to know what other people know. We must know for our survival.

Tiny Questions are innocent "yes" and "no" questions that we ask prospects for reminding them about their pain. Pain and pleasure are two motivators for getting prospects to make decisions. Most prospects will choose pain over pleasure.

Professionals will remind prospects about their pain without making them feel bad. Tiny "yes" and "no" questions remind the prospects about their pain. We don't want to rub salt in the wound, but we do want them to recognize their pain. Recognizing pain prompts a person to seek solutions.

We don't want to make our questions open-ended. Our tiny questions should be short and simple. They should be "yes" and "no" questions. Prospects will have no choice but to answer with a simple "YES" or "NO."

- I'm just curious. Does your skin get dry in the sun?

- I'm just curious. Do you like working 40-hour weeks?

- I'm just curious. Do you like work?

- I'm just curious. Do you like getting an extra paycheck?

- I'm just curious. Do you want to retire early?

- I'm just curious. Do you like living on your retirement income?

- I'm just curious. Don't you hate living on 60% of what you can't afford?

- I'm just curious. Do you like working weekends?

- I'm just curious. Do you like wholesale over retail?

- I'm just curious. Do you like to travel at discount rates?

- I'm just curious. Would you like to own your own business?

- I'm just curious. Do you like lower electricity bills?

- I'm just curious. Don't you hate waking up to acne every morning?

- I'm just curious. Do you hate joint pains?

- I'm just curious. Do you like free cell phone calls?

- I'm just curious. Do you like monitoring your heart?

- I'm just curious. Do you hate starving to death to lose a few pounds?

- I'm just curious. Do you like working as a waiter?

- I'm just curious. Do you like working at nights?

- I'm just curious. Do you like getting "yes-decisions from prospects?

- I am just curious. Do you like what you're doing?

- I'm just curious. Do you like getting healthy?

- I'm just curious. Do you like making money?

- I'm just curious. Are you married to your job?

- I'm just curious. Would you like to do something different?

What do we say when the prospects answer 'YES" to our tiny questions? **"Well, I Just Found Out How To" + "A Benefit that Soothes the Pain." + "If you'd ever like to know how, I'd be glad to show you."**

- Well, I just found out how to protect us against the sun by drinking this herbal tea. If you'd ever like to know how, I'd be glad to show you.

- Well, I just found out how to work part-time at full time pay. If you'd ever like to know how, I'd be glad to show you.

- Well, I just found out how to fire our boss and walk away with full pay. If you'd ever like to know how, I'd be glad to show you.

- Well, I just found out how to work part-time at home with full pay. If you'd ever like to know how, I'd be glad to show you.

- Well, I just found out how to get two extra paychecks a month without telling the boss. If you'd ever like to know how, I'd be glad to show you.

- Well, I just found out how to retire in 5 years at full pay. If you'd ever like to know how, I'd be glad to show you.

- Well, I just found out how to double our pensions in 9-months. If you'd ever like to know how, I'd be glad to show you.

- Well, I just found out how to live on what rich people can't afford. If you'd ever like to know how, I'd be glad to show you.

- Well, I just found out how to work two-days a week and get paid for five. If you'd ever like to know how, I'd be glad to show you.

- Well, I just found out how to sign up with this new business and get wholesale prices. If you'd ever like to know how, I'd be glad to show you.

- Well, I just found out how to travel first class at second-class rates. If you'd ever like to know how, I'd be glad to show you.

- Well, I just found out how to own our own business and not interfere with our week. If you'd ever like to know how, I'd be glad to show you.

- Well, I just found out how to make our electricity bills smaller and bank account bigger. If you'd ever like to know how, I'd be glad to show you.

- Well, I just found out how to clear acne once and never have to worry about it again. If you'd ever like to know how, I'd be glad to show you.

- Well, I just found out how to get the flexible joints of a 16-year old. If you'd ever like to know how, I'd be glad to show you.

- Well, I just found out how to get a smart phone with free calls. If you'd ever like to know how, I'd be glad to show you.

- Well, I just found out how to wear a watch that monitors our heart and pulse at the doctor's office while we work and play. If you'd ever like to know how, I'd be glad to show you.

- Well, I just found out how to lose 40 pounds in 22-days without starving ourselves to death. If you'd ever like to know how, I'd be glad to show you.

- Well, I just found out how to make more money part-time than our boss makes full time. If you'd ever like to know how, I'd be glad to show you.

- Well, I just found out how to work days part-time with full pay. If you'd ever like to know how, I'd be glad to show you.

- Well, I just found out how to get more "yes-decisions" from prospects than "no-decisions". If you'd ever like to know how, I'd be glad to show you.

- Well, I just found out how to work three months and get paid for twelve months. If you'd ever like to know how, I'd be glad to show you.

- Well, I just found out how to get healthy and get paid big money for it. If you'd ever like to know how, I'd be glad to show you.

- Well, I just found out how to make more money working at home part-time than you do working at your job full-time. If you'd ever like to know how, I'd be glad to show you.

- Well, I just found out how to change careers and make more money part-time than you make full-time. If you'd ever like to know how, I'd be glad to show you.

Notice we added the killer punch line at the end of each statement, "**If you'd ever like to know how, I'd be glad to show you.**" If the prospects find interest in what you have said, they will ask us to explain more. If the prospects are not interested in what we have said, no harm and no foul. The prospects will move on to another topic.

- "Mr. Prospect, I'm just curious. Do you like working at nights?"

- *Mr. Prospect* says, "No! It sucks."

- "Well, I just found out how to work days part-time with full pay. If you'd ever like to know how, I'd be glad to show you."

- *Mr. Prospect* says, "Wow! Tell me now!"

Here's another example.

- "Sue, I'm just curious. Do you like lower electricity bills?"
- Sue, says, "Yes!"
- "Well, I just found out how to make our electricity bills smaller and bank account bigger. If you'd ever like to know how, I'd be glad to show you."
- Sue replies, "Now is a good time."
- Want another example? Let's change it up.

Margie has just sent us a "Thank You" message for connecting on LinkedIn. We are in the health and wellness business. What should be our response?

- "Margie, I'm just curious. Do you like getting healthy?"
- Margie says, "Sure!"
- "Do you like making money?"
- Margie says, "Yes!"
- "Well, I show people how to get healthy and get paid big money for it. If you'd ever like to know how, I'd be glad to show you."
- "That sounds great, Dale. Tell me more."

Notice how I used two tiny questions instead of one. Then I added the "**I Show People How To**" benefit statement. It serves the same purpose as "**Well, I Just Found Out How To**" statement.

- Jim, do you like getting "yes-decisions" from your prospects?
- Jim says, "Of course! Who doesn't?"

- "Don't you just hate getting turned down by prospects?"
- Jim says, "Yes!"
- "Well, I show Network Marketers how to turn prospects who say "no" into prospects who say "yes.""
- If you'd ever like to know how, I'd be glad to show you."
- Jim says, "Let's talk."

Never ask more than four tiny questions. You don't want to turn a conversation into an interrogation. Four tiny questions are all we will need.

- "Billy, I'm just curious. Do you like living on your retirement income?"
- Billy says, "It's okay."
- "Do you miss playing golf since retirement?"
- Billy says, "Yes, but I can't afford it."
- "Don't you just hate living on 60% of what you can't afford?"
- Billy replies, "I certainly miss the income."
- "Well, I show retirees how to double their pensions in 9-months and afford playing golf every day. If you'd ever like to know how, I'd be glad to show you."
- Billy says, "Tell me more!"

See how the magic of ice-breakers work? Well, stay tuned. We have more.

FYI: Only after you've built rapport will ice-breakers work.

(4). Would it be Okay?

"Would It Be Okay If" is a magic phrase we can add to a benefit to create a great ice-breaker. **"Would It Be Okay if" + "A Benefit" = Ice-Breaker**.

Ever had your children come to you and say, "Daddy, would it be okay if I had some ice-cream?" "Momma, would it be okay if I went to the mall?"

And momma and daddy give in.

Why does it work? It's reasonable and it's polite.

When the subconscious mind hears, "would it be okay if," before a request, it answers with a "yes. Because this person is polite, and his request is reasonable, I can listen."

Want some examples?

- Would it be okay if you didn't have to go to work again?
- Would it be okay if you could retire in 5-years at full pay?
- Would it be oaky if you could make more money part-time than you could full-time?
- Would it be okay if you could schedule time on my calendar for us to talk?
- Would it be okay if you could make an extra paycheck?

- Would it be okay if you could double your pension in 9-months?

- Would it be okay if you could fire your boss and walk away with full pay?

- Would it be okay if you could work two-days and get paid for five-days?

- Would it be okay if you could if you could make your bills lower and your bank account higher?

- Would it be okay if you could buy a college instead of attending a college?

- Would it be okay if you could try this herbal tea to lose weight?

- Would it be okay if you could make your home toxin-free and safe?

- Would it be okay if you could wear a piece of jewelry that monitors your heart and pulse during work or play?

- Would it be okay if you could add more energy to your life?

- Would it be okay if you didn't have to burn in the sun again?

- Would it be okay if you could put more passion in your life day or night?

- Would it be okay if you could clear acne once and keep it off forever?

- Would it be okay if you could own your own business?

- Would it be okay if you could work from home with the hours that you choose?

- Would it be okay if you could help others and get paid for it?

- Would it be okay if you could get healthy and get paid big money for it?

- Would it be okay if you could heal damaged cells after a vigorous workout?

- Would it be okay if you could retire when you graduate college?

- Would it be okay if you could work from your home instead of commuting?

- Would it be okay if you had more holidays?

- Would it be okay if you had more vacation time?

- Would it be okay if you could buy a car without payments?

- Would it be okay if you could buy a home without a mortgage?

- Would it be okay if you could wipe your credit card debt clean?

- Would it be okay if you could lower your electricity rates?

This formula will create thousands of ice-breakers. **"Would It Be Okay If"** + **"A Benefit".** List all the benefits of your products, services and opportunities. Then add the appropriate ice-breaker.

How do you determine what is a benefit? If it can fix a problem, it's a benefit.

(5). Whiners and Complainers.

If you hear whiners and complainers, they set the stage for a great ice-breaker.

"Would you like to do something about it?"

When you hear people whine and complain about a problem, you can ask them, "**Would you like to do something about it?**"

Jim is on LinkedIn talking to a new prospect. Jim builds rapport and then the prospect opens to Jim about his job.

"It sucks! I have the late hours at the office. Lunch breaks are fifteen-minutes long. My coworker sitting to the right of me has bad breath. My boss? He is a real nag."

Jim, fresh off training with ice-breakers, says, "Would you like to do something about it?"

The prospect replies, "Yes, but what?"

What happened? The prospect has signaled for Jim to help him fix the problem.

Now, I can hear the whiners and complainers tell me, "Dale, all my friends are happy. They have no complaints. All is peachy clean. What do I do?" Well, we will induce negativity.

The next time you meet a cheery, happy-go-lucky Susan or Sam with no problems, you will say, "**What are the two biggest problems with _____?**"

- What are the two biggest problems with **your career**?
- What are the two biggest problems with **dieting**?
- What are the two biggest problems with **finances**?
- What are the two biggest problems with **working late at night**?
- What are the two biggest problems with **cleaning your home**?
- What are the two biggest problems with **retirement**?
- What are the two biggest problems with **your health**?
- What are the two biggest problems with **your job**?

Sit down, take pages of notes, because cheery, happy-go-lucky Susan and Sam are going to talk your ear off. They're not only going to talk about their present problems but about all the problems in their past. They'll even talk about problems they don't have. People love talking about their problems.

After happy-go-lucky Susan and Sam have talked your ear off, you'll have ten pages of notes. Then you can ask them, "Would you like to do something about it?"

So far, we've learned how to build trust, likeability and belief using the power of rapport. We've learned how to introduce our business into a conversation.

Want a real-life conversation on how it works on LinkedIn? This happened recently. I've changed the names to protect the guilty.

- **JUDE**: Mona, thanks for connecting with me. You're in Network Marketing. That's awesome. There's an old saying that everybody does Network Marketing every day, but they just don't get paid for it. Agreed?

- **MONA**: "LOL. That is so right. I agree."

- **JUDE**: "Most people want extra money, and most jobs don't pay enough. Network Marketing is the better alternative."

- **MONA:** "You couldn't be more right."

- **JUDE**: "What do you do for a living?"

- **MONA**: "I'm a secretary."

- **JUDE**: "Awesome! You must be natural at it."

- **MONA**: "I work for great bosses."

- **JUDE**: "I'm just curious. Do you like getting healthy?"

- **MONA**: "Yes!"

- **JUDE**: "Do you like making money?"

- **MONA**: "Of course, who doesn't?"

- **JUDE**: "Well, I show people how to get healthy and get paid big money for it. If you'd ever like to know how, I'd be happy to show you."

- **MONA**: "Sounds good. Could you clarify?"

- **JUDE**:

"Sure! Some people have more money than health. They are more than willing to spend a little bit of their money to reclaim their health. Everyone wants to live longer, healthier lives.

Other people have more health than money. They are willing to trade a little bit of their health to earn more money. They work overtime. They seek out part-time jobs. They even start part-time health and wellness businesses to earn more money. So, what do you think?"

- **MONA**: "I'd like to learn more."
- **JUDE**: "Would it be okay if we could schedule a time on my calendar for us to talk by telephone? You can schedule a time at your convenience. Want the link?"
- **MONA**: Send it. I look forward to it.

We see all the skills we've learned so far in one conversation. And the results? We've added a new team member.

There's nothing like offering one more option to help improve someone's life. We would have never been able to reach this person if it was not for learning skills.

Chapter 9:
Closing.

We have three more skills to master.

- Closing.

- Handling objections.

- Giving presentations.

Chapter 9 is dedicated to closing.

Closing happens before the presentation. Closing is getting yes-decisions before the presentation. The presentation confirms the prospect's yes-decision.

Want a real-life example? (Once again, I changed the names to protect the guilty).

Dale sends an invitation to connect and meets Keith. Dale is in Network Marketing. Keith is in Network Marketing. Dale is on LinkedIn to build his team. Keith is on LinkedIn to find a new Network Marketing career.

- **DALE**: You're in Network Marketing. That's awesome. There's an old saying that Network Marketing is all about making a decision and sticking with it. Sounds like you have made the decision to stick with it.

- **KEITH**: Been with it for 2-years.

- **DALE**: That's great. Most Network Marketers stick with it for getting an extra paycheck but fall short and then quit.

- **KEITH**: I've been there.

- **DALE**: Besides Network Marketing, what do you do for a living?

- **KEITH**: I fix computers.

- **DALE**. That's great. I bet you're a natural at it.

- **KEITH**: I do okay.

- **DALE**: I am just curious. What are the two biggest problems with repairing computers? People I know in your field say repairing computers is a challenge.

- **KEITH**: Competition is tough. Too many other computer repair people. Working odd hours.

- **DALE**: Are you okay with the competition and working odd hours?

- **KEITH**: I wish I had made better career choices.

- **DALE**: Sounds like a real problem. Can you do anything to fix it?

- **KEITH**: Not really. I'm too old to start a new job.

- **DALE**: If you could, would you like to do something about it?

- **KEITH**: Yes!

- **DALE**: I'm just curious. Do you like getting healthy?

- **KEITH**: Yes!

- **DALE**: Do you like making money?

- **KEITH**: Who doesn't?

- **DALE**: Would it be okay if you get healthy and get paid the big bucks for it? Then you won't have to go back working on computers again.

- **KEITH**: Yes!

- **DALE**: Well, I show people how to get healthy and make more money part-time than they make full-time with their job? If you'd ever like to know how, I'd be glad to show you.

- **KEITH**: What do you have?

- **DALE**: So, here Is the short story. Instead of working odd hours and hating your job for repairing computers, you could start with us. Then you can choose the hours you want to work and make more money part-time than you make full-time at your job.

- **KEITH**: I like it.

- **DALE**: Would it be okay if you could schedule time on my calendar to talk by telephone? You can schedule a time at your convenience. Want the link?

- **KEITH**: Yes, send it.

Dale used the full force of building rapport and breaking the ice. Did you catch these two skills in the message?

- **There's an old saying** that Network Marketing is all about making a decision and sticking to it.

- **What do you do for a living**?

- **Most Network Marketers** stick to it to get an extra paycheck but fall short and then quit.

- **You're a natural at it**.

- **What are the two biggest problems with** repairing computers?

- **Would you like to do something about it**?

- **I'm just curious. Do you like** getting healthy?

- **Do you like** making money?

- **Would it be okay if** you could get healthy and get paid big money for it so you would never have to go back to computer repair again?

- **Well, I show people how to** get healthy and make big money for it so they would never have to go back to work again? **If you'd ever like to know how, I'd be glad to show you.**

- **Would it be okay if** you could schedule time on my calendar to talk by telephone? You can schedule a time at your convenience.

Dale added one more skill. Closing!

What about the complete presentation? The complete presentation comes later. Dale used some statements before the presentation to close the prospect. He got the prospect ready for the presentation.

- "**Are you okay with** the competition and working odd hours?"

- **Sounds like** a real problem.

- "**Can you do anything to fix it**?"

We need to make three points about these three closing phrases and statements.

- They remind prospects of their pain.
- They limit the choices of the prospect.
- They offer the choice for fixing the problem.

It is our job to remind prospects about their pain. Sometimes that means, we must dig deep. Closing questions help prospects to uncover their hidden pain.

When we close, we want to offer two choices. We never want to take away from the prospects any of their choices. We want to limit their choices. Prospects can choose to keep their pain. Or, they can make the decision to move forward to fix their pain. Too many choices will confuse the prospect.

Two programs inside our subconscious minds motivate us.

- To seek pleasure.
- To avoid pain.

For example.

- If we have a hard time losing weight, we will compensate with overeating.
- If we don't have the time, we will engross ourselves into television shows or video games that take up too much time.
- If we procrastinate, we will find pleasure in staying where they are.
- If we don't have the money, we will overspend with credit cards.

Pain is the biggest motivator. It outperforms pleasure. Pain is the motivator that we will concentrate on. Make the pain big enough and the prospects will close themselves.

(1). Are You Okay With?

"**Are You Okay With**" is the polite way for focusing prospects on their pain.

- Are you okay with working 50-hour weeks?
- Are you okay with the boss yelling at work all the time?
- Are you okay with work interfering with time better spent at your son's baseball games?
- Are you okay with living on social security?
- Are you okay with a pension that is 60% of what you cannot afford?
- Are you okay with being in a job where raises never happen?
- Are you okay with being on the job for ten-years without a promotion?
- Are you okay with starving yourself to lose a few pounds?
- Are you okay with paying high electricity bills?
- Are you okay with smelling toxic chemical cleaners that harm your home?
- Are you okay with wages that limit the amount of vacation time you can afford?

- Are you okay with a bad heat left unmonitored by a doctor at work or play?

It is obvious. Prospects will feel the pain when we use the four magic words "Are You Okay With."

(2). Sounds Like. Feels Like. Looks Like.

"**Sounds Like**," "**Feels Like**," or "**Looks Like**" uncovers the pain by speaking to pleasure.

When I say to you, "Sounds like your job is a lot of fun," internal programs begin to work in the subconscious mind. If work is a lot of fun, you'll agree with me and let me know. Or, if work is not a lot of fun, you will disagree with me and let me know.

I meet Joe on LinkedIn. Joe tells me he works as an information technology person. I know nothing about IT guys. So, I say to Joe, "Sounds like your job is a lot of fun." Joe tells me differently. Joe lists three reasons why work is not fun.

- Unstable work hours.

- Shift work on weekends and holidays.

- The stress on the job.

By saying, "Sounds Like," I've uncovered Joe's pain. Want some other examples?

- Sounds like your job is a lot of fun.

- Feels like your diet is working for you?

- Looks like your home is toxin free?

- Sounds like your vacation was a lot of fun.

You get the idea.

(3). Can You Do Anything to Fix It?

"Can You Do Anything to Fix It?" gives prospects a choice. They can choose to stay where they are and wallow in their pain. Or, they can choose to move forward and fix their pain. Most prospects will realize they can't stay where they are. If they wish to fix their pain, they must be honest by answering the question with a "NO."

Mary meets Tracy on LinkedIn. Mary and Tracy are in Network Marketing. Mary closely follows her training on the five core skills of Network Marketing. Mary has built rapport. She has broken the ice. She has asked closing questions. The messages between Mary and Tracy are going great.

Mary has uncovered Tracy's pain. Tracy is not making any money with her company. She has been in Network Marketing five-years with only $200 for all five-years to show for her effort.

Mary asks Tracy, "Can you do anything to fix it?" Mary admits she cannot? What should Mary's response be?

"If you could, would you like to do something about it?'

Tracy says, "No!"

Mary must find out if Tracy is willing to fix her problems. If Tracy is not willing to fix her problems, Mary can't help her.

We want to speak only to people who are willing to move forward and not stay where they are. If people don't want to fix their problems, let them be and wish them the best. Then be on your way.

(4). The Million-Dollar Close.

Want a closing question that creates millionaires? It makes more money for Network Marketers than any other close. It is a simple, hype-free and no-pressure close.

"Well, what do you think?"

Want some examples?

- The cost is $65 for a 40-day supply that comes with a 30-day money back guarantee. So, that's about it. Well, what do you think?

- That's it. That's the whole explanation about our opportunity. Well, what do you think?

- Our training calls will be on Monday and Thursday nights at 7 pm central. That about wraps everything up. Well, what do you think?

Our prospects will tell us what they think.

- The cost for the products is reasonable and I love the money back guarantee. How do I pay for it? Cash, check or credit card?

- I like the opportunity. I can't pay for it until payday Friday. If that is alright with you, then let's do this thing.

- I am busy on Monday night for a wedding. But Thursday and each Monday and Thursday afterwards, I'm all in.

Prospects are not turned off by the million-dollar close. Prospects like the million-dollar close. They feel they we aren't pushing sales upon them. There is no salesy hype to the question. It's simple and gets right to the point.

(5). The Five Question Close.

Templates are great. They provide a way for people to be creative. They are not limited by what someone else has created. You are free to add your own stuff.

Five questions provide a template for closing.

- If There is a Way You Could + **Benefit #1** + **Benefit #2** + **Benefit #3**… you would at least like to know about it, wouldn't you?

- Have You Ever + **Previous Experience**.

- What Did You Like Most About Your + **Previous Experience**?

- What Did You Like Least About Your + **Previous Experience**?

- What is the Most Important Reason You Want to + **Motivation**?

Want some examples?

Weight loss.

- If there was a way for losing weight, energizing the body and sleeping well at night, you'd at least like to know about, wouldn't you?

- Have you ever dieted?

- What did you like most about dieting?

- What did you like least about dieting?
- What is the most important reason you want to lose weight?

Business Opportunity.

- If there was a way for firing the boss, making more money, and retiring in five years you'd at least like to know about it, wouldn't you?
- Have you ever considered a home-based business?
- What did you like most about a home-based business?
- What did you like least about a home-based business?
- What is the most important reason you want to work from home?

Legal Services.

- If there was a way for saving money on living wills, traffic violations and trusts, you'd at least like to know about it, wouldn't you?
- Have you ever considered legal services?
- What did you like most about legal services?
- What did you like least about legal services?
- What is the most important reason you want legal services?

Organic Cleaners.

- If there was a way for keeping your home, family, pets and the environment safe from toxic chemicals, you'd at least like to know about it, wouldn't you?

- Have you ever considered organic cleaners?

- What did you like most about organic cleaners?

- What did you like least about organic cleaners?

- What is the most important reason you want to try organic cleaners?

These are great questions to help you start a conversation. And you will be closing while you are messaging your connections.

(6). Closing at the End.

Closing is not always all about what happens before the presentation. We have to say something after the presentation.

Three questions we can ask to sum up the opportunity at the end of the presentation.

- What did you like best about what you saw and heard?

- Do you see yourself doing this business?

- Sounds to me like you're ready to get started?

Albert has just given a one-minute presentation. With his last word spoken about the presentation, Albert asks Larry, "What did you like best about what you saw and heard?"

Albert shuts up and waits for Larry's answer. Albert says he likes the extra money. He likes the car bonus program. And he especially likes the vacations.

Albert does not end the question there? Albert's next question is, "Is there anything else?"

Larry responds, "I think the weight loss products are exactly what I need." Larry shuts up, and Albert continues. "Anything else you can think of?"

Larry shakes his head "No."

Albert asks the second questions, "Do you see yourself doing this business?"

Larry says, "Yes, I know it is right for me."

Then Albert asks the final closing question, "Sounds to me like you are ready to ready to get started?" Albert shuts up. There is dead silence from Larry. Albert does not dare speak.

Then Larry says, "Yes, I am ready to get started."

Albert signs Larry to the team on the spot.

Why does this work? Larry is closing himself.

Larry is admitting all the reasons for why he wants to do this business. Extra money – car bonus – vacations – weight loss program. He has agreed to these benefits. It would be impossible for Larry to deny what he has just affirmed.

Albert asks Larry one question in three different ways.

- What did you like best about what you saw and heard?

- Is there anything else?

- Anything else you can think of?

The reason we ask this question three different ways is we want our prospects to sell themselves. The more good things they have to say, the more they'll affirm their decision to buy or join.

"Sounds to me like you are ready to get started" sounds to me like we are uncovering pain. If there is any hidden pain in the prospect, here is where we will find it. Here is where the objections will happen.

Chapter 10:
Handling Objections.

Agreement! Handling objections is to agree. We will agree with whatever objection the prospects throw at us. We won't prove them wrong. We won't make them feel bad for their reasoning. We will simply agree.

When someone agrees with us, it is hard for them to fight us. It is hard for them to object. We will agree with the prospects and then the prospects will be open to listen.

To get prospects to agree, we will use these words:

- "Relax."
- "It's okay."
- "Of course."
- "Yes, I see."
- "Correct."
- "Precisely."
- "Right."
- "Absolutely."
- "Exactly."

Prospects will start listening when we use words of agreement.

We are going to use a formula. "Relax, it is okay to make a decision not to [**insert that "no" decision**] and [**insert consequences**]. But it is also okay to make a decision to [**buy or join**] and [**insert benefit**]."

(1). I Don't Have Any Time."

Our prospects say, "I don't have any time for this business." What is our response?

- "Of course, you don't have any time. That is exactly why I'm talking with you now. You don't want this to be true for the rest of your life. Let's discuss some possibilities now, so that you will never be in that situation again."

- "Yes, I see you don't have any time. That is exactly why I'm talking with you now. Staying in that situation may be true for you now, but you don't want it to be true for the rest of your life. Let's get on the telephone now and discuss some possibilities so you'll never be in that situation again."

- "Absolutely you don't have any time. Who doesn't these days? That is precisely why I'm talking with you now. You don't want this to be true for the rest of your life. Let's discuss some possibilities so you'll never be in that situation again."

- "You're right about not having any time. All 24-hours of your day are used up already. So, what are you willing to sacrifice in your day that you can change your situation and have time for your family and yourself?"

We've spent 10-seconds turning a "no" into a "yes."

Agreement will pay off. Answer the first objection with agreement. Then any other objections in the prospects' minds will vanish. The subconscious mind of the prospect will say, 'This person agrees with me. So, I can let down my guard for any other resistance. He is on my side."

Want to see how it works with other objections?

(2). The Pyramid Scheme.

Network Marketers won't ask other Network Marketers if their business is a pyramid. But other people might. So, it's a good idea to nip this one in the bud.

There are two ways for dealing with it. One is the short way. The other is the long way.

The short way starts with the phrase "correct."

Susan says to Jim, "Is this one of those pyramid things?" Jim has the perfect answer.

"You're correct for bringing up this question. There's an old saying that everybody does Network Marketing every day, but they just don't get paid for it."

What has Jim done?

Jim agrees with Susan that bringing up the objection is a good idea. That neutralizes Susan's resistance.

- Jim uses the rapport builder "There's an old saying." This creates likability, believability and trust.

- The statement after "There is an old saying" handles the objection itself.

Jim further explains:

"You've purchased items from a store. You've recommended the same items to family and friends. Some of them bought these items on your recommendation. Did you get paid for it? No, but in Network Marketing you do."

The longer version goes like this:

"You're precisely right for bringing up this question. When you are working at your job, your boss is receiving earnings off the skills you have learned. What if your boss gave you better skills? Do you think your boss would make more money? Do you think your job would be better? Your boss would make more money, and you would make more money. Well, that is how our business works. The person who invited you into this business wants to train you with the skills for being successful. The only way they can earn money is for you being successful."

(3). I Need More Information.

The number one objection on LinkedIn is "I need more information?" Four statements will answer it.

Kelly gives a short presentation to Bill. Bill's natural response is, "I need more information."

Kelly responds with four statements.

- You're right for requesting the information.
- What would you like to know first?
- What would you like to know next?
- What would you like to do next?

Statement #1 agrees with Bill that his question is virtuous. Agreement is more virtuous than disagreement. Kelly agrees with Bill that it is right to bring up the question.

Question #2 will put the ball back in Bill's court. It forces Bill to bring up the real questions he might have.

Question #3 will dig deeper into Bill's objections. Most people have one or two questions. Answer the first one or two questions, and the "I need more information" statement shuts down.

Question #4 will turn Bill's "no" objection into a "yes-decision."

There is an alternative. We will refocus the prospect back to the question, "Do you want to start a business with me… or not?"

"If you enjoy gathering information, that is okay. But at some point, you will have to stop collecting information, stop putting off action and take your first step forward to start our business. You can collect information for years after you start our business, but we need to start it first. So, the real question that you and I have is this: Do you want to start a business now… or not?"

(4). Let Me Send You My Link.

Network Marketers love to send other Network Marketers their links. They want you to look at their stuff. Don't get mad. Accept the link. LinkedIn's creators made it for conducting business. Links to products, opportunities and services are part of having a business. On LinkedIn, you can send links. On Facebook, it is taboo.

Imagine if you are in Network Marketing and one of your connections sends a link. Her name is Julie. What would be the proper response?

"You are so correct for sending your link. I am passionate about the Network Marketing industry. I love to learn about other Network Marketing companies. Let's hop on a call because I'd love to chat with you about your company over Virtual Coffee. Here's my online scheduler, so you can setup a call at your convenience (**Link to Your Online Calendar**).

With the presentation skills you will be learning later in the book, you'll know exactly what to say to Julie.

(5). I'm Not a Sales Person.

You hear this objection all the time. I've heard other Network Marketers tell people there is no selling involved. The truth is Network Marketers must sell if they wish to make money.

So, how do we handle this objection?

"Of course, you are not a sales person. That is why I am talking to you now. The company doesn't want a bunch of old school, sleazy door-to-door salespeople promoting its products. They want real people like you and me sharing our experiences with others. Remember how you had an experience once in your past? Remember how it helped you for solving a problem? And how you shared it with other people for helping them to solve their problems? Well, that is what we do. We share the experiences that fixed our problems with other people for fixing their problems, and we get paid for it. That's better than being a sleazy salesperson. As a non-salesperson, this opportunity is made for people like you."

(6). I Don't Have the Money.

There are two ways to handle the objection.

List some **expenses** the prospect might have.

- Golf.
- Cable.
- Smoking.
- Eating out.
- Movies.
- Pizza.
- Manicures.
- The spa.

Then put the expenses in a formula.

- "It's Okay if You Don't Have the Money. You Have **(The Expense),** Right? "Which will make you more money? **(The Expense)** or Our Opportunity?"

- It's okay if you don't have the money. You play golf, right? Which will make you more money? Golf or our opportunity?

- It's okay if you don't have the money. You have cable, right? Which will make you more money? Cable or our opportunity?

- It's okay if you don't have the money. You like smoking, right? Which will make you more money? Smoking or our opportunity?

- It's okay if you don't have the money. You eat pizza, right? Which has a better chance for helping you lose weight? Eating pizza or our products?

- It's okay if you don't have the money. You get a manicure, right? Which will help for protecting your skin against the blistering sun? Getting manicures or our skincare product?

Spending money on one of these items tells the prospects they have money for spending on our offers.

The second way to handle the objection?

"Of course you don't have the money. That's why you are talking to me. You certainly don't want to be broke all your life. Let's get on the telephone and discuss some possibilities so you'll never be in that situation again."

(7). Your Product is Too Expensive.

- "I agree with you that our product is expensive. Our product is a treat or luxury. It's like spending money on dining out, having a manicure, lottery tickets, or beer."

- "You are right for saying our product is expensive. Our product is a treat or luxury. It's like spending money on golf, a day at the spa, buying stuff off Amazon, eating out with friends, or drinking at the bar."

- "Yes, it is expensive. The company wanted to make a cheaper version, but they knew it wouldn't work. And they didn't want to rip you off."

(8). I Don't Know Anyone.

"Of course you don't know anyone. That is why I am talking to you now. You don't want it to be the case for the rest of your life. Our company has a training program that will show you how to meet new positive people wanting what we offer. Plus, you will have me as a sponsor to help. So, let's get you started in the company now and enroll you for the training program right away."

(9). I Want to Think it Over.

- "Relax, it's okay for deciding not to start with our business today. And it's okay for continuing to work 45-years before retiring at a 60% cut in pay. It's also okay if you make the decision to start with us today and begin the countdown for retiring in 5-years at full pay instead."

- "Relax, it is okay to decide not to buy this energy drink and continue to let your body tire out during work or at home or play."

- "Relax, it's okay if you keep your current utility supplier and continue paying for the highest utility rates on the street."

- "Relax, it's okay if you decide not to buy our wearable technology today. It's also okay to continue risking your heart to irregularities without a doctor's 24-hour care."

(10). I Don't Know How to Do this Type of Business.

"Of course you don't know how to do this type of business. No one expects us to know how to work a business before we start. That would be silly. That is why the company has special training for helping you get started even if you have zero knowledge. Plus, you'll have me as your sponsor for helping you with every step of the way. So, let's sit down now and get you started, so we can get you enrolled in the company training program right away."

(11). Would You Front My Start-Up Cost?

Network Marketers won't ask you to front start-up costs. Other people might. You want a good answer.

"We can guarantee the skills for making you successful. We cannot guarantee that you will apply the skills for being successful. If you don't apply the skills, we don't get paid? That is why we don't front your startup cost."

(12). How Much Money Have You Made?

New team members will get this question. If you have not made any money, it is good to have an answer.

"None. It is a business. It will take 6-months for me to make a good profit. Then I am going to take a cruise for a week and relax. I just wanted to know if you would like to join me now, so we could take a cruise together. Or, if you would rather give me your address, I can send you a postcard from my cruise."

(13). How Does Your Pay/Compensation Plan Work?

This question is a trick question by some people. They hope you won't have a good answer. Here is the right answer.

"Well, if we have a lot of people using the products, we make a lot of money. If we have fewer people using the products, we make less money."

(14). What's the Catch?

Some people are skeptical. There are skeptical about the free gifts. They are skeptical about our offers. They are skeptical because they've been burned in the past. They will ask you, "What's the catch?" We should welcome skeptical people.

"It's okay if you're skeptical. Apparently, there is a story behind your skepticism. Would it be okay if you share it?"

(15). I'm not Interested.

"It's okay if you're not interested. That's why you are talking to me. Ironically, our business is made for people who aren't interested. But you do know people who are interested. Just point me to the people who are interested, and you can collect a pretty nice paycheck while you're still not interested."

(16). It's a Numbers Game and the Numbers are Against Us.

"You are correct. It's a numbers game. That's why my business cuts down the numbers and odds against us. Instead of talking to 10 wrong people and getting 10 "no-decisions," we'll talk to 5 right people and get 5 "yes-decisions." Let's sit down and I'll show you how."

Chapter 11:
Presentations

LinkedIn presentations will take two forms. One form is a short story. The other form is a detailed presentation. The detailed presentation takes form in a later chapter. The short story concerns us here.

We'll tell short stories for our prospects in LinkedIn messenger. We'll give detailed presentations by a video conference or telephone call.

Which sounds better for a prospect?

(**A**). "My presentation will take 30-minutes of your time. Could you spare 30-minutes?"

Or,

(**B**). "Here is the short story."

The answer is obvious.

Short stories are brief descriptions of our offers. They're glimpses into seeing the bigger picture for our opportunity, products and services. They are only summaries and not packed with a lot of detail. You won't find testimonies, facts, information, data, and boring bits that people hate.

Our goal is to chat with people through LinkedIn messenger. We will build rapport and introduce our offers into a social conversation. We'll handle objections. We will close and give a short-story presentation. Our short story gives a brief description for what we offer and represent.

The short-story prepares the prospect for what is to come. What a prospect knows about us from the beginning will prepare him for a detailed presentation at the end. So, if they like the short story and want more information, we can give the details later.

The short story formula? Five parts.

- "So, here is the short story."

- "Instead of" + [A Problem].

- "So, here is the short story."> + <"Instead of" + [A Problem].> + <"You could work/switch/use/start/ drink/take" + [Your business/service/product]> + <"A benefit that solves the problem]..

- "A benefit that solves the problem."

- The million-dollar close, "Well," before the word "What." It should read, "Well, what do you think?"

Want some examples?

- "So, here is the short story. Instead of working 40-years and retiring with a big cut in pay, you could work with us for 5-years and retire at full pay. Well, what do you think?"

- "So, here is the short story. Instead of eating donuts, you could drink one of our power shakes for breakfast and now you can manage your weight for the rest of your life. Well, what do you think?"

- "So, here is the short story. Instead of spending time away from your family because of a job, you could work with us and get paid big money for spending time with the family. Well, what do you think?

- "So, here is the short story. Instead of higher electricity bills with another company, you could switch to us with the same electricity and smaller bills. Well, what do you think?"

- "So, here is the short story. Instead of a physician keeping tabs on your health and draining your bank account, you could start with us and get healthy and make big money for it. Well, what do you think?"

- "So, here is the short story. Instead of working at a job with people that you don't like, you could work with our business and choose people to work with that you do like. Well, what do you think?"

- "So, here is the short story. Instead of attending college and racking up debt, you could start with us and buy a college and have no debt. Well, what do you think?"

- "So, here is the short story. Instead of graduating college and working 40-years like your parents, you could work with us and retire before you graduate. Well, what do you think?"

- "So, here is the short story. Instead of working 40-years hard labor like your parents, you could tart with us and retire in 5-years at full pay. Well, what do you think?"

- "So, here is the short story. Instead of spending money on jewelry for looking good, you could start with us and make money wearing techy jewelry that looks good and cares for your health. Well, what do you think?"

- "So, here is the short story. Instead of your children eating vegetables they hate, you can give them one of our tasty gummy bear tablets and get the nutrition of 16 vegetables a day. Well, what do you think?"

- "So, here is the short story. Instead of listening to your skin wrinkle in bed, you could use our cream every night and watch your skin look 16-years younger all over again. Well, what do you think?"

- "So, here is the short story. Instead of paying your mobile phone bill, you could use our credit card at local merchants and have them pay all your phone bill for you. Well, what do you think?"

- "So here is the short story. Instead of paying for coffee at a restaurant with zero health benefits, you can drink one cup of our coffee a day that tastes great, costs less and melts belly fat. Well, what do you think?"

- "So here is the short story. Instead of paying for coffee, you could start with us and make more money part-time for drinking our coffee than you make full-time at work. Well, what do you think?"

- "So, here is the short story. Instead of buying a home and accruing a mortgage, you could start with us and get bonus checks for a down payment and monthly installments for a new home. Well, what do you think?"

- "So, here is the short story. Instead of a down payment with monthly payments for a new car, you could start with us and have the company buy you a new car with no monthly payments. Well, what do you think?"

- "So, here is the short story. Instead of paying doctors for protecting your children from germs and viruses, you could try one of our drinks. Then you could save money from doctor bills and boost their immunity. Well, what do you think?"

- "So, here is the short story. Instead of working at a job full-time for limited pay, you start with our business and work part-time for unlimited pay. Well, what do you think?"

- "So, here is the short story. Instead of working for a boss draining your life away, you could start with us and fire your boss and walk away with full pay. Well, what do you think?"

- "So, here is the short story. Instead of having more health than money or more money than health, you could work with us and get paid more money and have better health. Well, what do you think?"

Our detailed presentation will be taken up later.

How about a conversation on LinkedIn messenger that shows off all our skills?

- **YOU**: Hey, John, thanks for connecting. I see you are with Ambit, the energy company that helps make your bank account grow bigger while your utility bills grow smaller. That is awesome.

- **JOHN**: I like it.

- **YOU**: How long have you been with them?

- **JOHN**: 2-years.

- **YOU**: I bet you're a natural at it.

- **JOHN**: I like the savings on my electricity bills.

- **YOU**: There's an old saying that if you de-energize your utility bills, you will energize your bank account. LOL! I'm not sure if it fits, but it sounds good.

- **JOHN**: LOL! I think it's cool. It fits.

- **YOU**: Besides Network Marketing, what do you do for a living?

- **JOHN**: I'm a director of a clinic.

- **YOU**: That's awesome. Sounds like a very interesting job.

- **JOHN**: It's okay! It keeps me busy and pays the bills. What do you do?

- **YOU**: I show people how to make more money part-time than they do full-time.

- **JOHN**: Really!

- **YOU**: Yep.

- **JOHN**: How?

- **YOU**: Later, what's more important is what's going on for you and your business, right?

- **JOHN**: My business is currently slow this time of the year. But I'd like to know more about your business.
- **YOU**: Okay, do you like drinking coffee?
- **JOHN**: Yep!
- **YOU**: Do you like making money?
- **JOHN**: Of course.
- **YOU**: Well, I show people how to drink coffee and make more money part-time than they make full time.
- **JOHN**: How much money have you made?
- **YOU**: None. It is a business. It will take 6-months for me to make a good profit. Then I am going to take a cruise for two weeks and relax. I just wanted to know if you would like to join me now, so we could take the cruise together. Or, if you would rather give me your address so I can send you a postcard from my cruise. The last part? Just kidding.
- **JOHN**: LOL! That's cool. But I'd love to go on a cruise. Well, I do like coffee and I like to make money. Can you tell me more about it?
- **YOU**: So here is the short story. Instead of paying for coffee, you could start with us and make more money part-time for drinking our coffee than you make full-time at work. The details for making money with it? We will have to talk about it later. Well, what do you think?

- **JOHN**: Sounds good. Drinking coffee and making money sound good to me. But I'd like to know more about it.

- **YOU**: Of course. Let's talk! Would it be okay if we could schedule a time to talk by telephone? I have an online calendar, so you can pick a time and date at your convenience. Want the link?

- **JOHN**: Yep.

- **YOU**: Here's the link (**The link to an online calendar**).

- **JOHN**: Thanks. I will schedule it today.

Conversations on LinkedIn messenger should be a pleasant experience. Learning the right skills can turn a pleasurable experience into a more pleasurable opportunity.

Chapter 12:
Let's Find People and Invite People to Connect

Starting conversations for Network Marketers is hard to do when you don't know where to begin. We are going to take baby steps.

Our first baby step will be to find people. Our second baby step will be connecting with people.

We are going to invite people. We are going to connect with people. We'll use a series of prefabricated messages for inviting people. We'll use prefabricated messages for connecting with people.

Starting conversations on Facebook is easy for building friends and relationships. Starting conversations on LinkedIn is harder.

Facebook makes it easy to build friends and relationships. Posting quotes, pictures or videos of your children's birthday parties is easy. They're great conversation starters.

LinkedIn is more about professionalism than about posting pictures and videos of family. LinkedIn is about building connections for business purposes.

So, we'll avoid posting cute pictures, quotes or videos. We will post things only for building business relationships.

Our conversations on LinkedIn will center around building business relationships.

What do we say to start? Our skills will help us with saying the right words.

Our first two baby steps?

· Step #1: Invitations.

· Step #2: Connections.

We will follow these two steps in sequence. It makes for a much smoother ride.

You're going, "Ugh! Ugh! That sounds too slow." Well, it is. Everything on LinkedIn moves slower than it does on Facebook. People do not spend hours a day on LinkedIn like they do on Facebook. They check messages about twice a week. They view posts sometimes three times a week.

Don't expect your invitations, messages or conversations to happen right away. They do not on LinkedIn. Sometimes you will wait days, and other times it will be weeks before you'll receive an answer.

But we can speed up the process. We will make things interesting. We will outthink the competition. We will grab the prospect's attention.

So, be patient. Your patience will pay off. So, let the conversations begin.

(1). Finding People.

We must find people before connecting with people.

To help us with finding people, we are going to need three tools.

First, head over to **Evernote.Com** and download the app both for your cell phone and your desktop computer. It's a free app. Free is always better. You can sync your cell phone and desktop with this app.

Second, head over and grab a free online scheduler at **Calendly.Com**. A more advanced online calendar for payment of a few dollars a month is at **Scheduleonce.Com**. If you have another calendar that you already use, it's okay too. Make sure people can click a link and setup a time for talking with you. If they cannot, you will need one of the two schedulers given here.

Third, we will need links to ten complimentary gifts. There will be more about the gifts later in this chapter.

We'll start building connections with other Network Marketers. Starting conversations with them requires little convincing on how great Network Marketing is. They're already convinced.

We need to find people to connect with.

To find people on LinkedIn, you will need the following directions.

Go to the search engine in the upper left-hand corner of your home page.

- Click the search engine.
- A drop-down menu appears. Click "**People**" from the menu.
- The "**People**" page appears. Click on "**All Filters**."

- The "**All People Filters**" page appears.
- Under "**Connections**," you'll click 2nd and 3rd connections.
- Ignore "**Connections Of**."
- Under "**Locations**," you'll type the countries where your search will begin. Only type country names where you speak the language and your opportunity operates.
- Under "**Profile Language**," you'll click the language that you speak.
- Under "**Current Companies**," you'll type the name for a Network Marketing Company. For example, you'll type "**Amway**."
- A drop-down menu will appear where you'll find a listing of all **Amway** groups.
- Choose each **Amway** groups in the list for your search.
- Now, click the "**Apply**" button in the upper right-hand corner.

FYI: You can't find the 2nd or 3rd connections and your language?

- Instead of moving from step #3 to step #4, you'll stop **after** step #3.
- Type ""**People**" in the search engine after step #3 and click the "**Enter**" button.
- Then you'll continue with steps 4 through steps 13.

Some accounts have a flaw. 2nd and 3rd level connections and languages sometime do not show. The extra step corrects the flaw.

Some of you may be saying, "I don't know any Network Marketing companies, so I can't do a search." Yes, you can do a search. You have "Google Search" to thank. Type "**Top Network Marketing Companies**" in the Google Search Engine. There you'll find a list of Network Marketing companies for searching. If you want a search by country, you'll type "**Top Network Marketing Companies + <the name of the country>**.

Once your search is complete, the first page of connections will appear. Each page will list 25 connections. Some of them will be blank. Others will have "Message" buttons. The only connections that concern us are the ones saying "**Connect**."

You can scroll to the bottom of the page and click the page number for advancing to the next page.

The level of your LinkedIn account limits the number of connections for any one day. For the non-paid version, it is 25 to 35 connections a day. For the paid version, it is 300 connections a day. LinkedIn will notify you when your limit is reached.

Our goal for the non-paid version is sending at least 25 connections. Thirty-five connections are better.

For the paid version, our goal is 300 invitations a day. Yes, that means 7-day weeks.

Does it mean we'll start conversations seven days a week? Yes! The more conversations that you'll start, the more business that you'll generate.

FYI: If you decide for the paid version of LinkedIn, buy the "**Business (Find Leads) Package**." Do not buy the "Sales Package." Unless you have purchased the "Sales Package" for other purposes, it will not work for our purposes.

(2). The Invitation to Connect.

Once we find people, let's connect. We will start with an invitation. An "**invitation to connect**" is asking someone to connect with us. We'll invite people to connect using LinkedIn's powerful invitation program.

LinkedIn's invitation program allows 300 characters to send an invitation to connect.

After connecting, one single message on messenger can be no more than 2,000 characters. We'll never send a 2,000-character message. For our purposes, it is fruitless and not necessary.

This is going to be a copy and paste operation. Open your Evernote app and click "**New Note**." The New Note window opens. In the subject line you will type "**Invitation to Connect**."

In the body of Evernote, you will type this message for **message #1**.

I came across your profile on LinkedIn, and I see you're in _____. I thought it would be good to connect. Would love to connect if you are open to it.

Thanks,

Your First Name

Below that, you will type another message for **message #2.**

I see you are in Network Marketing. I'd love to connect.

Looking forward to it.

Thanks,

Your First Name

For message #1, you'll fill in the blank with the name for the Network Marketing company that you have searched.

For message #2, there is no need for a name of the Network Marketing company searched. You'll send the message as is.

Do not put any links in this message. Don't try to be cute. Putting links in the invitation to the connect message is unprofessional.

Sign only with your first name. Don't make it so formal with a first and last name.

What about the prospects first name? Ignore it. There's no need for putting the prospect's first name in our "**Invitation to Connect**."

Pretty simple, right?

Now that our "**Invitation to Connect Message**" is in Evernote, we can begin to connect.

We will copy and paste the "**Invitation to Connect Message**" into the LinkedIn "invitation" window.

Remember how we find people on LinkedIn? Find people on LinkedIn and then follow these steps to send an "Invitation to Connect."

- Click on the first "**Connect**" button and the "**Invitation to Connect**" window opens.

- Click the "**Add Note**" button, and a "**Note**" window will appear.

- From Evernote, copy and paste the "**Invitation to Connect**" message into the "**Add Note**" window.

- Click "**Send Now.**"

Easy, right?

Follow the same procedure with all the people that have **Connect** buttons. Remember, ignore any **Message** buttons. For the non-paid version of LinkedIn, you will connect with no more than 35 connections. There are 25 connections on each page. So that amounts to 1-1/2 pages.

For the paid version, you'll send the "**invitation to connect**" message to 300 connections. That is 12 pages. With copy and paste, you'll find you can send 300 connections a day in about 20 minutes.

Chapter 13:
A Thank You Message for Connecting

After people connect with us, one of us must take the first step to build a relationship. We'll take the first step. He who fires the first shot will win.

You'll celebrate with people and you'll thank people. You'll celebrate peoples' birthdays, new work positions, and work anniversaries. You'll thank people for recognizing your birthday. You'll thank people for recognizing your new work position and your work anniversaries.

How do we start? We will start with some messages.

Ten pre-fabricated messages sent out over time will start the ball rolling.

- Thank You for Connecting Message.

- New Work Anniversary Message for Our Prospects.

- Work Anniversary Message for Prospects.

- Thank You Message for My Work Anniversary.

- Thank You Message for My New Work Position.

- Birthday Message for Prospects.

- Thank You Message for My Birthday.

- Endorsing Our Prospects' Skills Message.

- Thank You Message for Endorsing My Skills.
- The Welcome Email Message for My New Lead.

This chapter covers the "**Thank for You for Connecting**" message.

People spend less time on LinkedIn than on Facebook. Every time we send a message, the prospect will receive an email notification. Sometimes, it will be days before we'll see results. Sometimes, the results are immediate.

Our first message may not reach the prospect. Sometimes, it's our second or third prefabricated messages that make the prospect respond. Other times, it may take four to six of our ten messages before they'll respond.

Be assured a series of our prefabricated messages will one day reach them. Patience is a virtue.

What do we do when people accept our "**I**nvitation to Connect?**" We will send them our next message.

The prospects have accepted our "**Invitation to Connect**." Now what? We'll thank them for connecting.

Open Evernote. Click **New Note**. The **New Note** window opens. In the subject line type "**Thank You for Connecting**."

Using the five skills that we have learned, we are going to design our own brand in the message.

Our "Thank You for Connecting" message has six parts.

- Part #1: First Name.
- Part #2: The message.
- Part #3: The gift.

- Part #4: Schedule a time to talk.

- Part #5: The signature.

Part #1: First Name.

"First Name" is self-explanatory. We will put a placeholder in Evernote for the first name of each connection. Calling people by their first names has power. It draws their attention to our message.

Part #2: The Message.

We'll want to thank the prospect for connecting. We will make it interesting for the person to read.

Thank you for connecting. I do appreciate it. I see you are in Network Marketing. I'm excited for you. You've joined the ranks of the best in the business world.

- Thank you for connecting. You are part of an elite group found nowhere else. Network Marketers like yourself make it possible for ordinary people to be extra-ordinary.

- Thank you for connecting. Influencers are movers and shakers. You've chosen Network Marketing. You've chosen to influence many and save many more from crushing debt and bad choices. You are part of the ranks created for the elite. I commend you.

- Thank you for connecting. I am excited that you've chosen the world of Network Marketing. With low risk and little financial commitment, we give people a chance for a better life. You've chosen well.

- Thank you for connecting. You're in Network Marketing. That makes you a cut above the rest. Instead of taking orders from others for the rest of your life, you've decided to build your own dream. I commend you.

- Thank you for connecting. To find the right person, you have to become the right person. By choosing Network Marketing, you've made the decision to be the right person. You've done well by choosing the right business.

- Thank you for connecting. Choices make the person. You've made a great choice. You've chosen to earn 1% of 100 people's efforts rather than 100% of your own efforts. It's a wise move for influencing many. You've chosen Network Marketing. You've chosen well.

Part #3: The Gift.

For connecting we will want to give a gift to our prospects. Prospects love gifts. Gifts will guarantee our "**Thank You for Connecting**" message is well received. We'll need **nine different gifts** for giving away with our messages. Don't panic, all will make sense as you read the book.

Our gift is a lead magnet. A lead magnet offers a gift for the exchange of contact information. If you give me your name and email address, then I'll give you a complimentary gift. The gift can be a digital download. It can be a free PDF file, or a report. eBooks, whitepapers, videos work also. Training videos are most popular for Network Marketers on LinkedIn.

Our gift will be something we'll give away for free. Prospects love free gifts. We are not going to charge any money for the gifts.

Is there a way to charge money? Yes, but only after the prospect receives the gift. The website that hosts the gift can upsell the prospect after the prospect receives the gift.

What gifts do we give a Network Marketer? Gifts that solve Network Marketers' problems. You will want to share gifts that Network Marketers can use for helping build their business.

Where will you find the best gifts? Gifts made by you for Network Marketers are the best gifts. Training manuals, videos, PDF files, audio files and websites made by you always work best. Training videos get the best response.

Gifts by other people for Network Marketers work also. To find the best gifts, you may have to join a few affiliate programs for Network Marketers. A cost for joining may be required. Gifts for helping Network Marketers recruit and sell on LinkedIn are always welcomed.

Host sites for gifts that spam the prospects are not acceptable. You could lose your LinkedIn account if it turns out you were the cause. So, be cautious and give only gifts from host sites that are spam-free.

This book is not designed for showing you what gifts to give. Depending on your industry, you will have to decide what's best for your target audience.

We'll need to say something about the gift. You must include two messages about the gifts.

- The name of the gift.

- One or two benefits that the gift offers.

Want some examples?

- As a thank you gift for connecting, I wanted to give you a complimentary copy of + "**Name of the Gift**." If you're like me, you want to find the best leads and prospects for your business. This gift will turn LinkedIn into a prospecting machine. Professionals will be hungry for your business and begging you to join. Here is the link: (**The Link to the Gift**). So, enjoy!

- As a thank you gift for connecting, I wanted to give you a complimentary copy of a new report. Network Marketers are always seeking tools for helping them grow their business. Turning people who say "no" to our offers into people who say "yes" is a welcomed gift. Accept this complimentary gift "**Name of the Gift**." It provides a hack for turning "no's" into "yes" eight out of ten times. Download your copy here: (**The Link to the Gift**).

- For connecting with me, I wanted to give you a no-obligation gift. Network Marketers need sales. Many don't know how to make a sale. They're shy and don't want to talk to your friends or afraid to talk to strangers. Accept this complimentary training video "**Name of the Gift**." It will help you position your retail sales, so people are happy to buy. Learn exactly what to say to make your retail sales soar. Here is your gift: (**The Link to the Gift**).

- I appreciate you for connecting with me. For connecting with me, I wanted you to have a complimentary copy of "**Name of the Gift**." Prospects don't always listen. Making something interesting grabs their attention. Opening first sentences that are interesting will grab the prospect's attention. They will listen to you EVERY TIME. Now they will hear the good things about your offers. Enjoy your free copy. You can download it here: (**The Link to the Gift**).

- Thank you again for connecting with me. For connecting with me, I wanted you to have a complimentary copy of my newest audio file "**Name of the Gift**." LinkedIn is the home for professionals. They're great assets for helping you to build your Network Marketing business. Sometimes you can get intimidated by them. Other times you don't know how to approach them. Sometimes, you're at a loss for getting the ear of professionals. With this gift, professionals will be begging you for a presentation. You can download your copy here: (**The Link to the Gift**).

- For connecting with me on LinkedIn, I wanted you to have a complimentary copy of "**Name of the Gift**." The old school 1960's way for closing people doesn't work anymore. So, let's make closing work for the age of the internet. Accept this complimentary copy for getting prospects begging you to help them buy. So instead of selling with high-pressure closes, let's make the prospect want to buy. Accept this complimentary copy as my gift for connecting. Download your free report here: (**The Link to the Gift**).

- Connections on LinkedIn are important. I wanted to give you this gift "**Name of the Gift**" for connecting with me. I have created a training website made only for my connections on LinkedIn. There's no obligation on your part. Network Marketers will need to know how to build their business. If your prospects knew how to build a Network Marketing business on 15-minutes a day, would it help you? Of course, it would. More people would be willing to join your team. Accept this complimentary gift by downloading it here: **The Link to the Gift**).

Part #4: Schedule a Time to Talk.

We will want our readers to act. We'll want them to click on the link for downloading their complimentary gift. We will want them to also schedule a time to talk with us by telephone or a zoom call. The purpose of the telephone or zoom call is to give a detailed presentation.

There are three parts for scheduling a time to talk.

- The reason for the talk.
- A name designated for our talk-session.
- The call to action message.

Never give a call to action without giving the prospects a reason for acting. So, we will need an introductory statement giving the reason for scheduling a time to talk.

Rather than speaking about general statements, we will put a name to our talk-session. When something has a name, it will always stick in our heads better than something without a name. It must be a catchy name that holds their attention, and it must be in "quotes." "Quotes" will make it stand out.

- "Virtual Coffee Session".
- "Mastery Strategy Session".
- "Master Skills Talk".
- "Let's Chew the Fat Strategy Session".
- "Off the Clock Strategies".
- "Business after Business Strategy Session".
- "Hourly Mingle Strategy Session".

Want some examples for making it work?

- I'd love to connect with you to find out more about what's going on for you and your business. If you'd be open to connect over a "**Virtual Coffee Session**" by telephone, I'd be happy to chat with you. You can book a time on my online calendar here: (**The link to the online calendar**).

- We know our business is what gives us financial reward and time-freedom. I'd love to talk with you by telephone about what's going on for you and your business. I enjoy talking to Network Marketers from different niches. I'd be happy to chat with you over a "**Mastery Strategy Session**" by telephone. If you'd like to talk, you can book a time on my online calendar here: (**The link to the online calendar**).

- I love to talk about skills. It is important to communicate skills with each other in our industry. If it's okay with you, let's have a **"Master Skills Talk"** by telephone. You can schedule a time to talk at your convenience with my online calendar. Click here: (**The link to the online calendar**).

- We can't get enough information For helping our customers and prospects lose weight. I like communicating with other people in our industry. If you'd be open to a **"Let's Chew the Fat Strategy Session"** (Yes, the pun is well intended), we can talk by telephone. If it's okay with you, I have an online calendar to set a time that works for you. Here is the link: (**The link to the online calendar**).

- Strategy Sessions help Network Marketers to connect with one another. It helps us communicate better and talk to each other one-on-one about our industry. I'd love to chat with you about what's going on for you and your business. If you'd be open to an **"Off the Clock Strategy Session,"** by telephone or zoom, I'd be glad to talk. For your convenience, here is my online calendar. Pick a time that works for you. Click here: (**The link to the online calendar**).

- We don't want to waste a good connection. Connections on LinkedIn are for building business relationships. I like to chat with other professionals in our industry. If it's okay with you, let's talk by telephone over a **"Business after Business Strategy Session."** I'd love to talk about what's going on for you and your business. I have an online calendar for your convenience. Here's the link to the calendar: (**The link to the online calendar**).

- Network Marketers have great communication skills. It's important we talk to one another about our profession and industry. If you'd be open, Let's have an "**Hourly Mingle Strategy Session**" by telephone. We can talk about what's going on for you and your business. You can schedule a time at your convenience. Here's the link: (**The link to the online calendar**).

If you are at a loss for a name for your strategy session, give Google Search a try. Type "**Catchy Slogans for Network Marketing Strategy Sessions**" in Google Search. Then you'll wait for the results. It works.

Part #5. The Signature.

Every message we send must have a signature. Our "**Thank You for Connecting**" must contain our first name and only our first name. Don't be formal with a first and last name. Included with our signature are our telephone numbers and a link to our website. Blogs, videos, business opportunities, PDF files, audio files are acceptable. Something that you can sell is acceptable.

An example?

- Welcome.
- John
- Phone Number: XXX-XXX-XXXX
- My Website: (**The link to the website**).

- Now, we can put together the whole "Thank You for Connecting" message. We have all the information that we need.

Thank You for Connecting Message #1.

FIRST NAME,

Thank you for connecting. I do appreciate it. I see you are in Network Marketing. I'm excited for you. You've joined the ranks of the best in the business world.

As a thank you gift for connecting, I wanted to give you a complimentary copy of + "**Name of the Gift**." If you're like me, you want to find the best leads and prospects for your business. This gift will turn LinkedIn into a prospecting machine. Professionals will be hungry for your business and begging you to join. Here is the link: (**The Link to the Gift**). So, enjoy!

I'd love to connect with you to find out more about what's going on for you and your business. If you'd be open to connect over a "**Virtual Coffee Session**" by telephone, I'd be happy to chat with you. You can book a time on my online calendar here: (**The link to the online calendar**).

Welcome.

John

Phone Number: XXX-XXX-XXXX

My Website: (**The link to the website**).

Thank You for Connecting Message #2:

FIRST NAME,

Thank you for connecting. You are part of an elite group found nowhere else. Network Marketers like yourself make it possible for ordinary people to be extra-ordinary.

As a thank you gift for connecting, I wanted to give you a complimentary copy of a new report. Network Marketers are always seeking tools for helping them grow their business. Turning people who say "no" to our offers into people who say "yes" is a welcomed gift. Accept this complimentary gift "**Name of the Gift**." It provides a hack for turning "no's" into "yes" eight out of ten times. Download your copy here: (**The Link to the Gift**).

We know our business is what gives us financial reward and time-freedom. I'd love to talk with you by telephone about what's going on for you and your business. I enjoy talking to Network Marketers from different niches. I'd be happy to chat with you over a "**Mastery Strategy Session**" by telephone. If you'd like to talk, you can book a time on my online calendar here: (**The link to the online calendar**).

Welcome.

Sally

Phone Number: XXX-XXX-XXXX

My Website: (**The link to the website**).

Thank You for Connecting Message #3.

FIRST NAME,

Thank you for connecting. Influencers are movers and shakers. You've chosen Network Marketing. You've chosen to influence many and save many more from crushing debt and bad choices. You are part of the ranks created for the elite. I commend you.

For connecting with me, I wanted to give you a no-obligation gift. Network Marketers need sales. Many don't know how to make a sale. They're shy and don't want to talk to your friends or afraid to talk to strangers. Accept this complimentary training video "**Name of the Gift.**" It will help you position your retail sales, so people are happy to buy. Learn exactly what to say to make your retail sales soar. Here is your gift: (**The Link to the Gift**).

I love to talk about skills. It is important to communicate skills with each other in our industry. If it's okay with you, let's have a "**Master Skills Talk**" by telephone. You can schedule a time to talk at your convenience with my online calendar. Click here: (**The link to the online calendar**).

Welcome.

Billy

Phone Number: XXX-XXX-XXXX

My Website: (**The link to the website**).

Thank You for Connecting Message #4.

FIRST NAME,

Thank you for connecting. I am excited that you've chosen the world of Network Marketing. With low risk and little financial commitment, we give people a chance for a better life. You've chosen well.

For connecting with me, I wanted you to have a complimentary copy of "**Name of the Gift.**" Prospects don't always listen. Making something interesting grabs their attention. Opening first sentences that are interesting will grab the prospect's attention. They will listen to you EVERY TIME. Once you have their attention, they can hear the good things about your offers that you have to say. Enjoy your free copy. You can download it here: (**The Link to the Gift**).

We can't get enough information For helping our customers and prospects lose weight. I like communicating with other people in our industry. If you'd be open to a **"Let's Chew the Fat Strategy Session"** (Yes, the pun is well intended), we can talk by telephone. If it's okay with you, I have an online calendar to set a time that works for you. Here is the link: (**The link to the online calendar**).

Welcome.

Judy

Phone Number: XXX-XXX-XXXX

My Website: (**The link to the website**).

Thank You for Connecting Message #5.

FIRST NAME,

Thank you for connecting. You're in Network Marketing. That makes you a cut above the rest. Instead of taking orders from others for the rest of your life, you've decided to build your own dream. I commend you.

Thank you again for connecting with me. For connecting with me, I wanted you to have a complimentary copy of my newest audio file "**Name of the Gift**." LinkedIn is the home for professionals. They're great assets for helping you to build your Network Marketing business. Sometimes you can get intimidated by them. Other times you don't know how to approach them. Sometimes, you're at a loss for getting the ear of professionals. With this gift, professionals will be begging you for a presentation. You can download your copy here: (**The Link to the Gift**).

Strategy Sessions help Network Marketers to connect with one another. It helps us communicate better and talk to each other one-on-one about our industry. I'd love to chat with you about what's going on for you and your business. If you'd be open to an "**Off the Clock Strategy Session**," by telephone or zoom, I'd be glad to talk. For your convenience, here is my online calendar. Pick a time that works for you. Click here: (**The link to the online calendar**).

Welcome.

Trent

Phone Number: XXX-XXX-XXXX

My Website: (**The link to the website**).

Thank You for Connecting Message #6.

FIRST NAME,

Thank you for connecting. To find the right person, you must become the right person. By choosing Network Marketing, you've made the decision to be the right person. You've done well by choosing the right business.

For connecting with me on LinkedIn, I wanted you to have a complimentary copy of "**Name of the Gift**." The old school 1960's way for closing people doesn't work anymore. So, let's make closing work for the age of the internet. Accept this complimentary copy for getting prospects begging you to help them buy. So instead of selling with high-pressure closes, let's make the prospect wanting to buy. Accept this complimentary copy as my gift for connecting. Download your free report here: (**The Link to the Gift**).

We don't want to waste a good connection. Connections on LinkedIn are for building business relationships. I like to chat with other professionals in our industry. If it's okay with you, let's talk by telephone over a "**Business after Business Strategy Session.**" I'd love to talk about what's going on for you and your business. I have an online calendar for your convenience. Here's the link to the calendar: (**The link to the online calendar**).

Welcome.

Kristi

Phone Number: XXX-XXX-XXXX

My Website: (**The link to the website**).

Thank You for Connecting Message #7.

FIRST NAME,

Thank you for connecting. Choices make the person. You've made a great choice. You've chosen to earn 1% of 100 people's efforts rather than 100% of your own efforts. It's a wise move for influencing many. You've chosen Network Marketing. You've chosen well.

Connections on LinkedIn are important. They help build business relationships. I wanted to give you this gift "**Name of the Gift**" for connecting with me. I have created a training website made only for my connections on LinkedIn. There's no obligation on your part. Network Marketers will need to know how to build their business. If your prospects knew how to build a Network Marketing business on 15-minutes a day, would it help you? Of course, it would. More people would be willing to join your team. Accept this complimentary gift by downloading it here: **The Link to the Gift**).

Network Marketers have great communication skills. It's important we talk to one another about our profession and industry. If you'd be open, Let's have an "**Hourly Mingle Strategy Session**" by zoom or telephone. We can talk about what's going on for you and your business. You can schedule a time at your convenience. Here's the link: (**The link to the online calendar**).

Welcome.

Paul

Phone Number: XXX-XXX-XXXX

My Website: (**The link to the website**).

One message down, and eight more to go. Now, I can hear all the moaning and crying. All your moaning and crying needs to stop. You weren't the one having to write them in a book. I'm Just kidding.

Chapter 14:
The Notifications Messages.

Other messages will make sure at one time or the other that we will get through to our prospects on LinkedIn.

Starting a conversation on LinkedIn messenger is a process. Sometimes we will have to send several messages before the prospect will respond. One message for sending is the "New Work Anniversary Message for Prospects."

LinkedIn will alert you to the new status of people on the "**Notifications**" page.

We'll find several types of notifications.

- Work anniversaries.
- New work positions.
- Birthdays.
- People endorsing your skills.
- Skills you've endorsed for other people.

How to find the "**Notifications**" page? Click the "**Notifications**" button on your Home page. The "**Notifications Page**" will open. There you will find all the notifications.

You will need to check your notifications page daily. The more people that connect with you over time, the more that people will show up in the notifications page. It's the nature of numbers. Greater numbers of people connecting mean greater numbers of new notifications.

(1). The New Work Anniversary Message for Prospects.

People on LinkedIn change careers. Recognition for the change is a good way for connecting.

Our "New Work Anniversary Message" will contain a **link for our second gift.** There will also be a link for prospects to schedule a time on our calendar to talk with us at their convenience.

Open **Evernote**. Click on **New Note**. The New Note window will appear. In the subject line, you will type "**New Work Anniversary Message for Prospects**."

The structure for the message?

- First Name.
- The congratulatory message.
- The gift.
- The link for the online calendar.
- The signature.

(1). "**The First Name**?" "First Name" is self-explanatory. Use the first name and only the first name. If you come across people with titles such as Doctors and Professors, you will still use their first name. Believe me, calling someone by their first name on LinkedIn will get you respect.

(2). "**The Congratulatory Message**?" A simple, "**Congrats on your new position!**" is required.

(3). "**The gift**?" State the name of the gift, a benefit or two by the gift, and the link for the gift. Our gift must be different in every new message. Do not give the same gift twice.

Want some examples?

- "Celebration is in order. Changing to a new work position calls for celebration. To help you celebrate, I wanted to give you a complimentary copy of our new training video "**The Name of the Gift**." Speaking with better words will bring you a steady stream of qualified prospects. This gift helps fill that need for LinkedIn. Click here to download your copy: (**The Link to the gift**)."

- "There is an old saying that changing one job for a better job is like saying goodbye to an old life and hello to a new life. Celebration is in order. And for helping you to celebrate, I wanted to give you a gift. "**The Name of the Gift**" is a complimentary copy. Finding leaders is hard. Recruiting leaders is harder. This gift helps with hacks for finding and recruiting leaders for your business. Accept this gift of celebration. Here is the link: (**The Link to the gift**)."

- "I say we ought to celebrate. You are taking on a new job with new challenges and new rewards. Congratulations! For helping you to celebrate, I wanted to give you a gift. If you can tell a story, you can do Network Marketing. Accept a complimentary copy " "**The Name of the Gift**." It gives you formulas for how to tell stories and get your message across easier than telling facts. Here is the link: (**The Link to the gift**)."

"**The Link to the Calendar**?" Here are three possibilities.

- It is worthwhile to communicate with other people in the industry. If you have any questions over the "**The Name of the Gift**," I'd be happy to discuss them with you. Here is a link to my online calendar for a "Virtual Coffee Session for us to connect: (**The Link to the online calendar**).

- If you would like to discuss how you can find leaders to help build your business, I'd love to talk with you. Schedule a time for us to talk on my online calendar. Here is the link: (**The Link to the online calendar**).

- Story telling is an art. I have lots of stories to tell. If you'd be open to talking about how to use stories to build your Network Marketing business, let's talk. Book a time on my online calendar at your convenience. Here is the link: (**The Link to the online calendar**).

"**The Signature**?" It has the same structure as the "Thank You for Connecting Message"

- "**To your success!**" starts the signature.

- "**Your First Name**," "**Phone Number**" and "**Link to Your Website**" finishes the signature.

Want to see how it looks in Evernote?

New Work Anniversary Message #1 for Prospects.

FIRST NAME,

Celebration is in order. Changing to a new work position calls for celebration. To help you celebrate, I wanted to give you a complimentary copy of our new training video "**The Name of the Gift**." Speaking with better words will bring you a steady stream of qualified prospects. This gift helps fill that need for LinkedIn. Click here to download your copy: (**The Link to the gift**)."

It is worthwhile to communicate with other people in the industry. If you have any questions over the "**The Name of the Gift**," I'd be happy to discuss them with you. Here is a link to my online calendar for a "Virtual Coffee Session for us to connect: (**The Link to the online calendar**).

To your success!

Christine

Phone: XXX-XXX-XXXX

My Website: (**The link to your website**)

New Work Anniversary Message #2 for Prospects.

FIRST NAME,

There is an old saying that changing one job for a better job is like saying goodbye to an old life and hello to a new life. Celebration is in order. And for helping you to celebrate, I wanted to give you a gift. "**The Name of the Gift**" is a complimentary copy. Finding leaders is hard. Recruiting leaders is harder. This gift helps with hacks for finding and recruiting leaders for your business. Accept this gift of celebration. Here is the link: (**The Link to the gift**).

If you would like to discuss how you can find leaders to help build your business, I'd love to talk with you. Schedule a time for us to talk on my online calendar. Here is the link: (**The Link to the online calendar**).

To your success!

Benny

Phone: XXX-XXX-XXXX

My Website: (**The link to your website**)

New Work Anniversary Message #3 for Prospects.

FIRST NAME,

"I say we ought to celebrate. You are taking on a new job with new challenges and new rewards. Congratulations! For helping you to celebrate, I wanted to give you a gift. If you can tell a story, you can do Network Marketing. Accept a complimentary copy " "**The Name of the Gift.**" It gives you formulas for how to tell stories and get your message across easier than telling facts. Here is the link: (**The Link to the gift**)."

Story telling is an art. I have lots of stories to tell. If you'd be open to talking about how to use stories to build your Network Marketing business, let's talk. Book a time on my online calendar at your convenience. Here is the link: (**The Link to the online calendar**).

To your success!

Sussy-May

Phone: XXX-XXX-XXXX

My Website: (**The link to your website**).

(2). The Work Anniversary Message for Prospects.

People on LinkedIn have careers. It is fitting for celebrating an anniversary for holding onto a job year after year.

We will need a link for a **third gift**, and we will need the link for our online calendar. Remember, we will give our prospects a new gift with each new message.

Open Evernote and click "**New Note.**" In the "**New Note**" window, type "**Work Anniversary Message for Prospects**" in the subject line. Here is our message for **Evernote**.

FIRST NAME,

Congrats on your work anniversary!

Celebration is in order. If you're like me, you stick to it through thick and thin. Congrats! To help you celebrate I'd like to give you a gift. Accept this free PDF File "**The Name of the Gift.**" It will make your follow-up efforts with prospects effective and rejection-free. You can download your complimentary copy here: (**The Link to the gift**).

People in our industry have much to give each other. If you have questions about this gift, let's chat by telephone over a "Virtual Coffee Session." You can set the time with my online calendar. Click here to find a date that works for you: (**The Link to the online calendar**).

Congrats!

James

Phone: XXX-XXX-XXXX

My Website: (**The Link to your website**).

(3). The Thank You Message for My Work Anniversary.

We'll have our own work anniversaries. People will send us congratulatory messages. Our response? A thank you message with a gift.

We will need a link for a **fourth gift** and once again the link for our online calendar.

Open **Evernote** and click "**New Note**." Type in the subject line "**Thank You for My Work Anniversary**."

Our message?

FIRST NAME,

Thank you for recognizing my work anniversary. I appreciate it very much. I was updating my profile. My updated profile will recruit people for my business while I sleep. My profile leverages the power of LinkedIn for building my Network Marketing business.

Again, I do appreciate your "thank you" message. To help me celebrate, I want to give you a gift. You know how we're always getting more "no-decisions" than "yes-decisions?" Well, I show people how the power of LinkedIn can turn every "no-decision into a "yes-decision." Accept this complimentary gift "**Name of the Gift**." You can download a copy here: (**The Link to the Gift**).

We belong to a unique industry. It's important for us to communicate with each other about our industry. I'd like to know more about what's going on for you and your business. Let's set up a "**Virtual Coffee Session**" so we can talk by telephone. Here is the link to my online calendar so you can pick the time: (**The Link to the online calendar**).

To your success!

Billy-Joel

Phone: XXX-XXX-XXXX

My Website (**The link to my website**).

(4). The Thank You Message for My New Work Position.

Like other people, we like to change our jobs. When we change our jobs, we will receive "Congratulation Messages" from our connections.

For every "Congratulation Message" that we will receive, we will send a "Thank You Message with a gift."

We will need a link for a **fifth gift** and the link for our online calendar.

Open Evernote and click "**New Note.**" When the "**New Note**" window opens, you will type "**Thank You for My New Work Position**" in the subject line.

Our message?

FIRST NAME,

Thank you for your congratulations message. It means a lot to me. I was adding a new set of skills for my profile. The more skills we learn for Network Marketing, the more people we can recruit.

I want you to celebrate with me. I have a complimentary copy on the five core skills for Network Marketing. You'll learn how to build rapport and introduce your business into a conversation. You'll learn how to close and handle objections. Most important you'll know what to say for giving the perfect presentation. "**Name of the Gift**" is a free PDF File and you can download here: (**The Link to the Gift**).

We both have unique skills. It's important for people in our industry if we talk about what skills work and why. If you'd be open to chat, let's talk by telephone soon. You can schedule a time at your convenience over a "**Virtual Coffee Session**." Here is a link for my online calendar: (**The Link for the online calendar**).

Thank you once again,

Billy-Rae

Phone: XXX-XXX-XXXX

My website: (The Link for your website).

(5). The Birthday Message for Prospects.

Open **Evernote** and click "**New Note**." The "**New Note**" window will open. In the subject line, you will type "**Birthday Message for Prospects**." Here is the birthday message for Evernote.

We will need a link for a **sixth gift** and the link for your online calendar.

FIRST NAME,

The great thing about getting older is that you don't lose all the other ages you've been. I love birthdays and I love celebrating birthdays.

My birthday is special, because I want to give you a gift. We all need good habits. This gift helps you focus on achieving three easy habits for attracting prospects. You can download your copy of "**Name of the Gift**" here: (**The Link to the gift**).

Celebrating your day with you!

Curtis

PS: If you have any questions about this program, I'd be happy to chat. Let's talk by zoom or telephone over a "**Business after Business Session**." If it is okay with you, let's schedule a time to talk at your convenience. Here my online calendar: (**The Link to the online calendar**).

Happy birthday again!

Curtis

Phone Number: XXX-XXX-XXXX

My Website: (**The link to my website**).

(6). The Thank You Message for Remembering My Birthday.

We do get older and we do have birthdays. Our connections will be sending us messages of "Congratulations" for our birthdays. So, let's have a "Thank You Message" for them.

We will need a link for a **seventh gift** and the link for our online calendar.

Open Evernote and type "**Thank You for Remembering My Birthday**" in the subject line.

What's the message?

FIRST NAME,

Thank you for remembering my birthday. I know giving gifts is the norm, but I'd like to break tradition. Instead of you giving a gift to me, let me give one for you.

Tiny innocent questions are the best way to get instant "yes-decisions." I have a report on the tiny questions you can ask your prospects to make more sales for your business. Accept this "**Name of the Gift**" by clicking here: (**The Link to the gift**).

I'm always looking to talk with people in our industry. If you're open to a "**Virtual Coffee Session**," let's chat by telephone about what's going on for you and your business. You can schedule a time at your convenience with my online calendar. Here's the link: (**The Link to the online calendar**).

Dale

Phone Number: XXX-XXX-XXXX

My Website: (**The link to my website**)

(7). The Thank You Message for Endorsing My Skills.

We will get our share of endorsements from our connections. We must have a "Thank You Message" for them. A link for a **ninth gift** and the link for our online calendar is necessary.

So, open Evernote and click **New Note**. In the subject line, you will type "**Thank You for Endorsing My Skills Message**."

Our message?

FIRST NAME,

Thanks for endorsing my "**Name of the Skills Endorsed**." You must be a natural at helping people. Your profile shows it.

For endorsing me, I'd like to offer you a gift "**Name of the Gift**." You can download it here: (**The Link to the gift**). This is a superior manual for helping you tell stories and reach multilevel success.

I like learning from other people in our industry. If you are open, let's talk by telephone over "**Virtual Coffee**." Schedule a time at your convenience with my online calendar. Here is the link: (**The Link to the calendar**).

Pauly,

Phone: XXX-XXX-XXXX

My Website: (**The link to my website**).

(8). Endorsing the Prospects' Skills Message.

We'll endorse other peoples' skills. Every time we will endorse a skill for someone, we'll send them a message.

Open "**Ever Note**" and click "**New Note**." Type "**Endorsing the Prospects' Skills Message**."

FIRST NAME,

I Just endorsed you for some new skills. I know this boosts your profile for others to see on LinkedIn. So, hopefully, it will help you.

To add an additional skill for your business, I want to offer you this gift. It's a complimentary copy "**Name of the**

Gift" for helping grow your downline in 4-steps. You can download your copy here: (**Link for the Gift**).

The one thing most Network Marketers lack is skills. They are missing the skills for getting the job done. I'd love to connect with you by telephone to find out more about what's going on for you and your business. It's worthwhile to connect with other people in our industry about our skills. If you'd be open to a "Virtual Coffee Session" so we can talk, here's the link for my calendar. Choose the time that works for you: (**Link for the calendar**).

Looking forward to it,

Billy-Rae,

Phone: XXX-XXX-XXXX

My Website: (**Link for your website**).

(9). The Welcome Email Message for My New Lead.

We will get leads. We'll need an email message for greeting the new leads. We will need a **tenth gift.** This gift will make us money. Our message will recommend and promote items for sale. This email message gives us a chance for cashing in on our hard work.

So, open Evernote and click "**New Note**." In the subject line, you will type "**Endorsing the Prospects' Skills**."

Our Message?

FIRST NAME,

I see you picked up a copy of (NAME OF THE LEAD MAGNET). Congrats! I've found the information in it helpful.

I've been in the network marketing business for over 10 years. I'm so thrilled to find tips and tricks for making network marketing work using the power of LinkedIn. I recommend this "**Name of the Sale Item**" if you're serious about growing your business. It's only $47 and there's a 30-Day guarantee, so you have nothing to lose. You can get it here: (**The Link to the gift**).

If you have any questions about this program, I'd be happy to chat with you over "**Virtual Coffee.**" Feel free to book a time on my online calendar here: (**The Link to the online calendar**).

Welcome again!!

Madeline,

Phone: XXX-XXX-XXXX

My Website: (**The link to my website**).

Chapter 15:
Let's Chat.

We've taken two baby steps. We've created copy and paste prefabricated messages. We've invited and connected with our prospects.

Now, it's time to grow up and take two giant steps.

- Step #1: Conversations.
- Step #2: Presentations.

Conversation is the third step. We will have to say something to get anywhere. What we will have to say builds on what skills we have learned. The five skills that we have learned will help us converse with the right words.

The presentation is the fourth and final step. It's the final step for getting people across the finish line. Getting people across the finish line is the conversion of "no-decisions" into "yes-decisions." It will take giving a detailed presentation for convincing people to convert.

This chapter is for conversations. The last chapter gives us the detailed presentation.

Our conversations are where we will have to put our skills to practice. The more we use the skills we have learned, the more natural for us it'll be.

Our five skills?

- Building rapport.

- Breaking the ice.

- Closing.

- Handling objections.

- Giving presentations (short stories).

Tom sent Bill an "Invitation to Connect" message. Bill did not respond.

The next day Tom got a notification for Bill's birthday. So, Tom sent Bill a "Happy Birthday" message. Bill did not respond.

Bill's work anniversary was the following week. So, Bill sent Tom a "Work Anniversary Message." Bill finally responds to Tom. Bill's response? A "Thumbs Up" icon in LinkedIn messenger. Bill never messaged any words of "thank you."

Should Tom reach out to Bill or ignore him? Tom should reach out to Bill and start a conversation.

Anytime we get a "Thumbs Up," an "Emoji," or other icons, we should start a conversation. Icons are signals for starting conversations.

Of course, words in LinkedIn messenger are always our first choice. It makes starting conversations so much better.

What do we say? Words that control the conversation.

He who controls the message will win. He who loses control of the message will lose. We will control the conversation.

How?

We'll make statements that are interesting and ask tiny innocent questions. Questions control the conversations.

There are five parts for a conversation.

- Open with first sentences.
- Answer in opposites.
- Uncover the Pain.
- Tell a short story.
- Ask for a time to talk.

(1). Open with First Sentences.

It is hard to start a conversation with "hello" and transition to "do you want to look at my business opportunity?"

Let's look at ways most Network Marketers start conversations with their prospects.

- "Hi, how are you?"
- "It's a great day."
- "How's the family?"
- "What did you do last weekend?"
- "Did you see last night's football game?"
- "Are you married?"
- "Do you have any children?"
- "Where are you from?"
- "What's new?"
- What's happening?"

These are useless opening first sentences. They're not comfortable transitions from saying "hello" to "join my business."

We want to start out of the gate talking about what every person loves talking about. Themselves!

Since we are talking to Network Marketers, we'll talk their language. Every Network Marketer loves talking about their Network Marketing business.

- Which works better for you? "Hey John, I see you are in Network Marketing?" Or, "Hey John, I'm glad you are part of an elite group that helps ordinary people to earn extra-ordinary income?'

- Which works better for you? "Hey Susan, I see you are in skincare?" Or, "Hey Susan, I see you are like me. You believe in helping people look younger?"

- Which works better for you? "Johnny, thank you for connecting?" Or, "Johnny, thank you for connecting. I see you've dropped out of the rat race where the rats are winning. You've joined the elite ranks of winners with Network Marketing?"

What happened with our opening first sentences?

- They are interesting.
- They greet the prospects.
- They build rapport.
- They control the prospects' thinking.
- They create for a smoother transition.

Our goal? We'll start with a greeting. We'll follow with a benefit. Then we'll ask if the prospects will empathize.

Want some good opening first sentences?

- Thank you for connecting. I see you're in Network Marketing. That's awesome. It's refreshing to meet people who have started their own business with no overhead.

- It's good meeting you. I see you're in Network Marketing. That's awesome. I see that you've learned the secret for getting a raise without telling the boss.

- Thank you for that "thumbs up." I see you're in Network Marketing. That's awesome. It's a pretty good day when I meet people who've learned how to fire the boss and walk away.

- It's nice meeting someone like yourself. I see you're in Network Marketing. That's awesome. At least you know what Network Marketing is about. It's one good opportunity away from being broke.

- It's great meeting you. I see you're in Network Marketing. That's awesome. At least you know the value of free vacations for life.

- It's nice meeting you. I see you're in Network Marketing. That's awesome. I looked at your profile. It reminds me of the caddy who started his own part-time Network Marketing business. He now owns the golf course.

- It's great meeting you. I see you're in Network Marketing. That's awesome. At least you understand what Network Marketing is about. Everybody does Network Marketing every day, but some people don't get paid for it.

- Thanks for connecting. I see you're in Network Marketing. That's awesome. There is an old saying that Network Marketing success is all about sticking with it. It looks like you've made the decision to stick with it.

- Thanks for connecting. I see you're in Network Marketing. That's awesome. You've at least figured out how to wake up every morning and not go to work. I wish more people understood it.

- Hey Jane, thanks for connecting. I see you're in Network Marketing. That's awesome. Like you, I found out how to have more holiday time with the family. I wish more people could experience it.

(2). Answer in Opposites.

What's our response to the prospects who agree with our opening first sentences? We'll answer in opposites.

Most prospects will agree with our opening first sentences. Our response? We'll speak about a negative followed by a benefit and an exception. The exception is the person we're chatting with.

Do we have a formula? Yes!

- "Most Network Marketers fail to stick with our type of business."

- "They start out wanting" + "a benefit" + "but they fall short and then quit."

- "I'm glad you're the exception."

Let's look at an example.

- **YOU**: It's great meeting you. I'm glad you are part of an elite group that helps ordinary people to earn extra-ordinary income.'

- **PROSPECT**: Yep! I learned it a while back.

- **YOU**: "Most Network Marketers fail to stick with our type of business. They start out wanting to help ordinary people to earn extra-ordinary income. but they fall short and then quit. I'm glad you're the exception."

Want other examples?

- "Most Network Marketers fail to stick with our type of business. They start out wanting to help people look younger with their products, and they fall short and then quit. I'm glad you're the exception."

- "Most Network Marketers fail to stick our type of business. They start out wanting to fire the boss and walk away, but they fall short and then quit. I'm glad you're the exception."

- "Most Network Marketers fail to stick with our type of business. They start out wanting to drop out of the rat race and join our elite ranks, but they fall short and then quit. I'm glad you're the exception."

- "Most Network Marketers fail to stick with our type of business. They start out wanting a business with low overhead and little cost, but they fall short and then quit. I'm glad you're the exception."

- "Most Network Marketers fail to stick with our type of business. They start out wanting pay raises without begging the boss, but they fall short and then they quit. I'm glad you're the exception."

- "Most Network Marketers fail to stick with our type of business. They start out wanting to build their fortune, but they fall short and then quit. I'm glad you're the exception."

- "Most Network Marketers fail to stick with our type of business. They start out wanting a few free vacations for life, but they fall short and then quit. I'm glad you're the exception."

- "Most Network Marketers fail to stick with our type of business. They start out wanting their own part-time business, but they fall short and then quit. I'm glad you're the exception.

- "Most Network Marketers fail to stick with our type of business. They start out recommending Network Marketing to other people, but they fall short and then quit. I'm glad you're the exception."

- "Most Network Marketers fail to stick with our type of business. They start out wanting an extra paycheck for paying bills, but they fall short and then they quit. I'm glad you're the exception."

- "Most Network Marketers fail to stick with our type of business. They start out wanting to wake up every morning and not have to go to work, but they fall short and then quit. I'm glad you're the exception."

- "Most Network Marketers fail to stick with our type of business. They start out wanting to get more holiday time with the family, but they fall short and then quit. I'm glad you're the exception."

- "Most Network Marketers fail to stick with our type of business. They start out wanting health and money with their wellness business, but they fall short and then quit. I'm glad you're the exception."

What will be their response to the exception?

- Yes, I am the exception.

- No, I'm not the exception.

- Yes, I'm living up to the benefit.

- No, I'm not living up to the benefit.

What's happened? We're stating a fact that is negative and true. We follow with the exception. We're building rapport and searching for their pain.

In our opening first sentence we are giving a positive message. Our second statement is a negative message.

Survival is necessary for the human condition. We want protection from harm. We want what makes us secure. "Most Network Marketers" is a magic phrase talking survival talk.

"Most Network Marketers" added at the beginning of a negative statement creates conflict. Internal programs are talking to us. It's asking,

"How can I associate with 'Most Network Marketers' who do the opposite for my survival?"

It causes conflict. Conflict means there is a problem needing a solution for survival.

Other internal programs are working. A positive statement followed by a negative message adds pain to an existing problem. Most people associate with their pain. They will seek pain over pleasure. The more pain they do feel, the more solutions they will seek.

And the exception?

Calling the prospects an exception will get one of two reactions.

- The prospects are the exception.

- The prospects are not the exception.

Most Network Marketers know they are not the exception. They unfortunately won't admit it. The "exception statement" increases their pain. It focuses them into realizing a problem exists. Only then can we help them to solve the problem. If people don't recognize they have a problem, we can't help them.

(3). Uncover the Pain.

We'll start the transition for relieving the Network Marketers' pain.

Most Network Marketing is part-time. Network Marketers have full-time jobs. Network Marketing for them is a side-project.

Most Network Marketers hate their jobs. They'd like Network Marketing to be full-time. They were never taught the skills for making it work full-time.

How do we get Network Marketers to reveal their pain? We must increase pain and make pleasure more desirable. We must increase the pain for working a job. We must make working Network Marketing more desirable.

People love pain more than pleasure. Don't believe me?

We meet a person who has joint pain. You've got a product made for the pain. We offer the solution, and the person says "no." "I like my pain because my kids will stop visiting if I don't keep the pain."

We meet a person who is overweight. We offer a solution and the person says "no." "I like being overweight because I hate exercising and I love eating fast food."

We must make the pleasure for working Network Marketing more desirable than the pain for working a job.

What do we say? We will make some statements. We'll ask a series of questions. We will use all our skills.

- **"Besides Network Marketing, what do you do for a living?"**

People love talking about themselves. Jobs are part of who they are. Talking about themselves is talking about their jobs.

Jobs are the source of pain for Network Marketers. We will talk about their jobs for uncovering their pain.

- **"You must be a natural at it."**

Our next statement is simple. We will complement their job. Most Network Marketers hate their jobs. Complementing the prospects' jobs will give you a hint on how they feel about them.

Other alternatives are:

- "Sounds like a great job."
- "Looks like a fun job."
- "Feels like you like what you are doing works."

The prospects will respond one of two ways.

- My job is great.
- My job sucks.

If the prospects' jobs suck, we will know there's a problem. If the prospects' jobs are great, we may or may not know there is a problem, but we can inquire further.

- **"I'm just curious. What are the two biggest problems with _____? People that I know in your field say _____ can be challenging."**

Want some other examples?

- "I'm just curious. What are the two biggest problems with **cleaning homes**? People I know in your field say it can be challenging."
- "I'm just curious. What are the two biggest problems with **repairing computers**? People I know in your field say it can be challenging."
- "I'm just curious. What are the two biggest problems with **banking**? People I know in your field say it can be challenging."
- "I'm just curious. What are the two biggest problems with **coaching**? People I know in your field say it can be challenging."

If the prospects say their jobs are great, the question here will uncover any pain. If the prospects say their jobs suck, here is where we will find why their jobs suck.

If the prospects do reveal more than one job, ask them, **"Which job do you spend more time on?"** The job where they do spend most of their time is the job where we will focus on the most.

We will add "**People that I Know in Your Field Say It's Challenging**" at the end of the statement. Adding this statement relaxes the prospect. They will feel less like an interrogation and more like it is everyday conversation.

- **"It's safe to say you're not okay with _____? (REPEAT BACK THE TWO PROBLEMS)."**

Our goal? Make the pain big enough so the prospects will be willing to do something about it to fix it.

We will repeat the problems that the prospects do reveal. Repeating the prospect's problems reminds them about the seriousness of their pain.

Want some more examples?

- "It's safe to say you're not okay with working long hours and no time for the family?"

- "It's safe to say you're not okay with little money to spend at the end of the month and no time left to enjoy for yourself?"

- "It's safe to say you're not okay with being away from your kids and falling behind each month with the bills?"

And to add some light-heartedness to the statement, we could say,

"That's like asking the hen if she'd like to do something about the fox nipping at her tail feathers. Lol."

It's just a bit of country humor.

- **"Sounds like it's a problem. Can you do anything to fix it?"**

We will need to know if the prospects have a solution to fix their problems. If they don't, we will want to know so when we do offer a solution, it will be well-received.

If they do have a solution? It will help us to avoid conflicts in solutions we offer with the solutions they've found.

If the prospects say they do have solutions to fix their problems, our next words will be, "**That's awesome! I assume your solutions are working well for you.**" Here the prospect will reveal whether their solutions are working.

Another alternative to the question? ""Would it be okay if you did something different to fix the problem?"

- **"If you could, would you like to do something about it?"**

This question transitions from "can you fix the problem" to "do you want to fix the problem." if they can't fix the problem but they want to fix the problem, we can help them.

If they have solutions for fixing the problem but their solutions fall short, we can still help them.

If they don't want to fix their problem, we can't help them.

- **"I'm just curious. Do you like getting _____?"**

We are asking a Network Marketer if he's happy with his job staying where he is. Most Network Marketers are not.

Their answers for the question are revealing.

Other tiny questions we could ask?

- "Do you like making money?"
- "Do you like getting healthy?"
- "Are you married to your job?"

Tiny questions can be endless. Remember, we'll want our tiny questions to be yes or no questions.

- **"Would it be okay if you could get _____ and make big money for it?"**

We're asking a Network Marketer if he would like change. Some Network Marketers like staying where they are. They resist change.

If they resist change, then we will know they are not open to a new business or product. We can't help them beyond here.

- **"Well, I show people how to _____ and make more money part-time than they make full-time. If you'd ever like to know how, I'd be glad to show you."**

Here we'll reveal the benefit for choosing our opportunity.

We are not pushing our opportunity. We are asking the prospect for permission to proceed with further information.

If the prospect doesn't want to proceed, he'll move forward to another subject. If the prospect wants to proceed, he will grant us permission to do so.

- **So, here is the short story. Instead of Problem #1 + Problem #2, you could start with us. Then you could get _____ and make more money part-time than you make full-time and never have to worry about going back to work again. Well, what do you think?**

If the prospect wants us to proceed with more information, we'll give them a presentation.

Our short-story should start with the prospect's two problems and end with one or two benefits.

We'll tell them a short-story. The short-story is a summary of what benefits we offer by joining us.

- **"Would it be okay if if we could schedule time on my calendar for us to talk by telephone? You can schedule a time at your convenience. Want the link?"**

Our prospects want details. We'll give them details with a detailed presentation. A detailed presentation is a series of questions with a two-minute story at the end.

A detailed presentation is what we'll use for qualifying the prospect for our offers.

Giving prospects a choice for a detailed presentation guarantees for a captive audience. Offering a prospect the link to our calendar assures us the prospect will hear our message.

If the prospect gives us permission for the link, we will send him a link for our calendar.

(4). Tell Me a Short Story.

An earlier chapter gives us the formula for creating short stories.

- "So, here is the short story."
- "Instead of" + [A Problem].
- "You could work with/you switch to/you use/you start with/you drink/you take" + [Your business/service/product].
- "A benefit that solves the problem."
- The million-dollar close, "Well, what do you think?"

Short stories sum up our offers. They should be glimpses into the bigger picture. They only give enough detail for the prospect to find interest. If the prospect is interested, he can ask for more detail.

(5). Ask for a Time to Talk.

Our calendar is a very important piece of the conversation. We don't want to force a time on our prospects. Let the prospects choose their own time for talking.

You'll find if you let the prospects choose the date and time, your closing rates will soar.

(6). A Real Conversation.

Want a real-life conversation to illustrate?

- **YOU**: It's nice meeting you. Your profile reminds me of a story. It reminds me of the caddy who started his own part-time Network Marketing business. Now, he owns the golf course. (**Opening first sentences**).

- **PROSPECT**: LOL. That is pretty good.

- **YOU**: I like it. Most Network Marketers fail to stick with our type of business. They start out wanting to build their fortune, but they fall short and then quit. I'm glad you're the exception. (**Speaking in negatives**).

- **PROSPECT**: I try hard to be.

- **YOU**: Besides Network Marketing, what do you do for a living? (**Rapport**).

- **PROSPECT**: I'm a hairstylist.

- **YOU**: You must be a natural at it. (**Rapport**).

- **PROSPECT**: That's very kind. Thank you.

- **YOU**: I'm just curious. What are the two biggest problems with styling hair? People that I know in your field say styling hair it can be challenging. (**Closing**).

- **PROSPECT**: My two biggest problems? Standing all day on my feet and getting paid with tips that are less money than what's paid by customers at other places. I work in a poor neighborhood. So, money is tight.

- **YOU**: I see. It's safe to say you're not okay with standing on your feet all day and getting paid less money in tips than what's paid elsewhere. (**Closing**).

- **PROSPECT**: Of course not.

- **YOU**: Sounds like they are big problems for you. Can you do something to fix them? (**Closing**).

- **PROSPECT**: No, not currently.

- **YOU**: If you could, would you like to do something about it? That's like asking the hen if she'd like to do something about it with a fox nipping at her tail feathers. Lol! (**Closing**).

- **PROSPECT**: Lol! Yes!

- **YOU**: I'm just curious. Are you married to your job? (**Closing**).

- **PROSPECT**: It's not much fun right now. So, no!

- **YOU**: Would it be okay if you did something different to fix the problem? (**Closing**).

- **PROSPECT**: Yes, but what?

- **YOU**: Do you like getting healthy? (**Closing**).

- **PROSPECT**: Yes!

- **YOU**: Do you like making money? (**Closing**).

- **PROSPECT**: Yes, of course!

- **YOU**: Would it be okay if you could get healthy and make more money part than you make full-time at your job? (**Closing and breaking the ice**).

- **PROSPECT**: Sounds great. But how?

- **YOU**: Well, I show people how to get healthy and get paid more money part-time than they make full-time at their job. If you'd ever like to know how, I'll be glad to show you. (**Breaking the ice**).

- **PROSPECT**: I'd like to know how.

- **YOU**: So, here is the short story. Instead of standing on your feet all day and working for poor tips paid with less money than what others pay, you could start with us. Then you could get healthy and get paid big money for it and walk away from your job. Well, what do you think? (**Short-story presentation and closing**).

- **PROSPECT**: I like it. Now what?

- **YOU**: Would it be okay if you could schedule time on my calendar for us to talk over the telephone? You can schedule a time at your convenience. Want the link? (**Invitation**).

- **PROSPECT**: Send it and I will schedule a time.

- **YOU**: Give me a second to grab the link.

- **PROSPECT**: I forgot to ask. How do you get paid?

- **YOU**: Well, if we have a lot of people using the products, we make a lot of money. If we have fewer people using the products, we make less money. (**Handling objections**).

- **PROSPECT**: Fair enough. Send the link to the calendar. And thanks.

- **YOU**: Here is the link and you're welcome. (**LINK**).

Chapter 16:
Detailed Presentations.

We will give detailed presentations. We will never give a detailed presentation unless the prospect will ask for it.

Our prefabricated messages contain links for our calendars. Our conversations contain links for our calendar.

Our prefabricated messages may or may not trigger a conversation. Prefabricated messages that start conversations are great. Prefabricated messages that don't start conversations are okay too.

The prospects will click on the links for our calendars and set an appointment. This may happen in a conversation. Or, it may happen outside of a conversation.

The links for our calendars let the prospects set a time for us to give a detailed presentation.

There are eight steps for giving detailed presentations.

- Step #1: Build rapport.
- Step #2: Set the framework.
- Step #3: Paint a picture of the prospects' dreams.
- Step 4: Paint a picture of the here and now.
- Step #5: Identify the gaps.
- Step #6: Bridge the gaps.

- Step #7: The close.
- Step #8: The referral.

Take a spiral ring notepad and open a fresh new page. Draw a line down the middle. On the left-hand side of the line, you will write "DREAMS." On the right-hand side of the line, you will write "HERE AND NOW."

Get ready to take notes as we progress through giving the presentation. You will need the prospects answers for the series of questions you'll be asking. Their answers will serve for helping us to close.

Step #1: Build Rapport.

We'll open our presentations with words for building rapport. We'll connect with the prospects who didn't have any conversation with us. We'll also reconnect with the prospects who did have conversations with us.

We'll always be in rapport with our prospects. Stating facts that are believable, likable and true will build rapport. We'll get the prospects on our side.

How do we start with people who didn't first converse with us?

Prospects whom we know nothing about make appointments with us. So, it's only natural for us to ask about the purpose of the appointment.

"Hey FIRST NAME, thanks for connecting with me. So, what's going on for you and your business?"

The question defines where we'll start our detailed presentation. It will leave open for where it will end.

The opening sentence defines the limits of the telephone call. You will want to keep the start of the conversation limited to what's going on for the prospect and his business.

The statement gives the prospect control. Giving control to prospects builds rapport.

What should you say next?

- "How long have you been with the company?"
- "Where would you love to be in your business?"
- "How many customers do you have?"
- "Have many team members do you have?"
- "Where would you like to be with your business in 12 months?"
- "Are your customers and team members sticking with it or dropping out?"

Be sure to write down the answers on the "HERE AND NOW" side of the paper.

But what about people with whom we've started conversations?

We know already what the telephone call is all about. We've prepared the prospects in our conversations for hearing the detailed presentation. There's no surprises for what the telephone call is all about.

So, what do we say next? What do we say next for people with conversations? We can start with:

"FIRST NAME, with all the offers that are out there, you must feel like you're stepping into a Baskin Robbins Ice Cream Store. There are 31 flavors to choose from and it can get confusing. Well, I am here to remove the confusion and give you **one option** for helping you make money for your bills. Is that okay?"

If you don't like that one, you can try this one:

"FIRST NAME, most of the time we get to pick and choose what we want in life. Sometimes the pickings are so slim that we are left with only a few choices. Sometimes the pickings are so plentiful that the choices can get confusing. Well, I am here to remove the confusion and give you **one option** for helping you lose weight. Is that okay?"

Want some more examples?

- "FIRST NAME, with all the offers that are out there, you must feel like you're stepping into a Baskin Robbins Ice Cream Store. There are 31 flavors to choose from and it can get confusing. Well, I am here to remove the confusion and give you **one option** for helping you fire your boss. Is that okay?"

- "FIRST NAME, most of the time we get to pick and choose what we want in life. Sometimes the pickings are so slim that we are left with only a few choices. Sometimes the pickings are so plentiful that the choices can get confusing. Well, I am here to remove the confusion and give you **one option** to choose for helping make your skin look younger. Is that okay?"

- "FIRST NAME, with all the offers that are out there, you must feel like you're stepping into a Baskin Robbins Ice Cream Store. There are 31 flavors to choose from and it can get confusing. Well, I am here to remove the confusion and give you **one**

option for helping you **take vacations at wholesale**. Is that okay?"

- "FIRST NAME, most of the time we get to pick and choose what we want in life. Sometimes the pickings are so slim that we are left with only a few choices. Sometimes the pickings are so plentiful that the choices can get confusing. Well, I am here to remove the confusion and give you **one option** for helping you get **healthy and make big money for it**. Is that okay?"

What's our formula?

- "FIRST NAME, with all the offers that are out there, you must feel like you're stepping into a Baskin Robbins Ice Cream Store. There are 31 flavors to choose from and it can get confusing. Well, I am here to remove the confusion and give you **one option** for helping you + **A Benefit.** Is that okay?"

- "FIRST NAME, most of the time we get to pick and choose what we want in life. Sometimes the pickings are so slim that we are left with only a few choices. Sometimes the pickings are so plentiful that the choices can get confusing. Well, I am here to remove the confusion and give you **one option** for helping you + **A Benefit**. Is that okay?"

Giving the prospects only **one option** will build rapport and put them at ease. Giving them too many options will create resistance to our message.

What happens next? We'll wait for agreement.

We'll wait for the prospect to agree with our opening sentences.

After agreement, what do we say next?

- We can all agree that starving yourself to death just to lose a few pounds is difficult. From what you've told me, what you're looking for is a way for helping you lose weight once and keeping it off forever. Did I get it right?

- We can all agree that strict dieting is impossible. From what you've told me, what you're looking for is a way for helping you eat the foods that you want while you lose weight. Did I get it right?

- We can all agree that a holiday with your mother-in-law isn't what you want. From what you've told me, what you're looking for is a five-star holiday at an affordable price. Did I get it right?

- We can all agree that traveling for you is expensive. From what you've told me, what you're looking for a way for helping you travel wholesale. Did I get it right?

- We can all agree that you want to live longer and dying is an inconvenience. From what you've told me, what you're looking for is a convenient way for living longer and living well. Did I get it right?

- We can all agree that you can't rich working a job. From what you've told me, what you're looking for is a convenient way for owning your own business. Did I get it right?

- We can all agree that today's equipment that monitors your heart is an inconvenience. From what you've told me, what you're looking for is a way for monitoring your heart while you're on the go at work and play. Did I get it right?

- We can all agree that working a job interferes with your life. From what you've told me, what you're looking for is a way for working two-day weeks and getting paid for five-days. Did I get it right?

- We can all agree that working at a job limits your income. From what you've told me, what you're looking for is a way for making more money part-time than what you make full-time. Did I get it right?

- We can all agree that you want to fire your boss and walk away. From what you've told me, what you're looking for is a convenient way for walking away from your job with full pay. Did I get it right?

- We can all agree that you want to get healthy and make big money for it. From what you've told me, what you're looking for is a convenient way for making more money and having better health. Did I get it right?

- We can all agree that credit card debt makes your stress levels bigger. From what you've told me, what you're looking for is a way for making more money a month than our credit card bills. Did I get it right?

Notice the formula? It's three sentences.

- "We can all agree that" + [A Problem Spoken About in Our Conversations].
- "From what you've told me, what you're looking for is a way for" + [A Solution Spoken About in Our Conversations].
- "Did I Get It Right?"

"**Did I get it right?**" will prompt the prospects to correct anything that we may have forgotten. Extra information comes out with this question.

What do we say next? Step #2.

Step #2: Set the Framework.

Setting the framework for where the presentation is heading helps for building rapport. It eases tensions. It eliminates resistance against our message.

The prospect will know what questions we will ask during the presentation.

So, what do we say? Six statements.

- "I would like to set the framework for our conversation."
- "First, I'd like to ask you a few questions to find out what your dream life would look like."
- "Then I'll ask you some questions to find out what's going on your life now–the good, the bad and the ugly."
- "Then we'll identify any gaps."

- "Then I'll tell you a little bit about what is I'm doing, and we'll explore whether this might be a fit for you."

- "Does this sound okay?"

Now, the prospect will know what they can expect. It makes for smoother presentation.

Step #3: Paint a Picture of the Prospects' Dreams.

Next, we are going to ask the prospects a series of questions. We will want them to focus on their dreams.

Vision boards are great tools. Vision boards help prospects paint a picture of what their perfect life would look like.

Instead of looking at pictures, we'll help them focus on building their dreams. We will help them focus on their dreams by using their own words.

We'll need to know the difference between "needs versus wants." There is a huge difference between needs and wants.

- Everybody needs to visit the dentist every six months. Do we want to? No!

- We all need to get up early and exercise. Do we want to? No!

- We all need to diet, eat healthy foods and stay away from pizza, ice cream and Mexican food and all the other food groups. Do we want to? No!

- We all need to pay taxes. Do we want to? No!

It's normal for people to need things but not want them.

What if we could find what everybody needs and wants? There are sixteen desires that **every person needs and wants**.

- Acceptance. We all need and want recognition and appreciation.

- Curiosity. We all need and want knowledge for meeting our curiosity.

- Eating. We all need and want food.

- Family. We all need and want what it takes for protecting our family.

- Honor. We all need and want the customs and values of our ethnic group, family or clan.

- Idealism. We all need and want social justice.

- Independence. We all need and want to be distinct and self-reliant.

- Order. We all need and want better preparation for established conventional environments.

- Physical activity. We all need and want physical activity for keeping us busy or exercising

- Power. We all need and want control over our will.

- Romance. We all need and want to romance the opposite sex and have sex.

- Saving. We all need and want things.

- Social contact. We all need and want relationships.

- Social status. We all need and want social significance.

- Tranquility. We all need and want what makes us secure and protected.

- Vengeance. We all need and want to strike back at others who do us or our family harm.
- Lucky for us, we can reduce all sixteen needs and wants to five passions that everybody hungers for.
- Companionship and love.
- Money.
- Desire for something great to be famous.
- Sex.
- Respect and admiration from others.

Five desires are the cream of the crop for satisfying everybody's appetite. So, we'll center our Dream Board around the five most common desires that everybody has a passion for.

In today's world, what stands at the forefront of everybody's needs and wants?

- Home. We all need and want the companionship and love of our family protected by a safe home.
- Travel. We all need and want money to be mobile.
- Family. We all need and want respect and admiration from others in our family.
- Health and fitness. We all need and want to be healthy and fit for romance and sex.
- Giving back. We all need and want to do something great to be famous.

Spending habits show what people love the most. People spend more money on a safe home, travel, health and fitness, and being famous than they do for other things.

Network Marketing companies focusing more on these spending habits make the most money.

Many of you may wonder why "jobs" are not on the list. It's because "jobs" belong to the "Here and Now." Dreams belong to the prospects' futures. We'll discuss jobs in the next step "The Here and Now." Jobs for many of our prospects are a necessary evil for the "here and now." Working at a job is not what their dreams would look like.

Here we'll want the prospects to only talk about what's important for them and their futures.

People will do anything for anyone who uses words to:

- Ease their pain.
- Encourage their dreams.
- Confirm their thoughts, concerns and feelings.
- Engage and capture their attention.
- Make them feel loved.
- Make them feel needed and significant.
- Give them a sense of hope.
- Make them feel they are contributing/leaving a legacy.
- Tell them secrets.
- Give them a sense of power.
- Offer a scapegoat.
- Calm their fears and doubts.

Which works better for convincing people something is true and works? Convincing people by our words? Or, someone's own words for convincing themselves?

The answer is obvious. People who convince themselves by their own words will close themselves.

We will only control the questions. Our questions will offer ways for the prospects to explain in their own words why they'll buy or join.

So, what do we say?

- "Tell me what your dream life looks like. Let's say there's an island of your Full Potential, or the island of your dreams. It's a place where everything is great and wonderful. What's your life like here? Can you do that for me?"

Then, we will follow with:

- "Can you paint me a picture of your dreams? For example, ... If money and time were not a problem, what would you do? What would you want?"

Then jump right into the questions for the five most common desires of all people.

Take notes on the DREAM side of your notebook.

- "HOME...."

"What would your dream home look like? Where would it be? (KEEP ASKING, 'Is there anything else?" until they can't tell you anymore)."

"Would you like a second home anywhere?"

- "TRAVEL..."
  - "Where would you like to travel if time and money were no object?"
  - "Is there any specific place in **REPEAT THE LOCATION** where you'd like to go?"
  - "Is there any place else you'd like to go?"
  - "If time and money were no object, would you like to travel first class?"
  - "Do you like travel to be adventurous, or do you like it slow and easy?"
- "FAMILY..."
  - "If you had all the time and money you wanted, would you spend more time with family and friends."
  - "Is there anything you would like to do with, or for, your kids?"
  - ... "Your partner/spouse?"
  - ... "Your parents?"
  - ... "Other family members and friends?"
- "HEALTH AND FITNESS..."
  - "Are there any ways in which you would like to improve your health and fitness?"
  - "Are you keeping your body energized at work or play?"

- "What are some the ways you maintain your weight, if any?"
- "Anything else you'd like to talk about for your health and fitness?"
- "GIVING BACK/CONTRIBUTING..."
  - "If time and money were not object, are there any ways for which you would like to give back? Or, ways for contributing to society or your community?"
  - "Are there any organizations you'd like to volunteer for, or help with?"

We will allow the prospects to answer each question. Write down the answers on the DREAM side of your piece of paper for taking notes.

Want some examples our prospect gives for the "Island of their Dreams?"

- "Coach sports in the local community."
- "Have four children."
- "A new Ford Explorer with all the bells and whistles."
- "Large 7-bedroom home on Florida's Cocoa Beach with 8 full baths."
- "Second home on Lake Ontario with 7-bedrooms and 8 baths."
- "Travel to Vienna, Austria and San Diego to see the famous zoo."
- "Mission trips to Haiti."
- "Travel first class."

- "Eat healthier."
- "Exercise more."
- "Join a gym and hire a personal trainer."
- "Lose 30 pounds."
- "Maintain strong relationships with my wife, children, family and friends."
- "Time freedom to travel at whim without the worry of cost."
- "Make sure my wife and children have everything they need."

Step #4: Paint the Picture of the Here and Now.

Step #4 gets easier. We will ask the prospects to answer questions by a scale of 1 to 10.

On the HERE AND NOW side on the piece of paper for taking notes, you will list the following:

- Finances.
- Career/job/business.
- Home.
- Health and fitness.
- Relationships with partner/spouse.
- Children.
- Other family.
- Friends.
- Time freedom.
- Anything else.

Our prospects for our next statements will answer questions on scale of 1-10. You'll write the number corresponding with the list on the HERE and NOW side of the notepad

What do we say?

"Now, tell me about the Island of the Here and Now. What does your life look like now? What is the good, the bad and the ugly? Do you mind if I ask you a couple of questions?"

- "On a scale of 1-10, with 1 being "**Horrible**" and 10 being "**Fantastic**," how happy are you with your finances?"

- "On a scale of 1-10, how satisfied are you with your career or job/business?"

- "On a scale of 1-10, how happy are you with where you live right now? The home you live in?"

- "On a scale of 1-10, how happy are you with your health and fitness?"

- "On a scale of 1-10, how happy are you with your relationships with:"

- ... "On a scale of 1-10 for your partner/spouse?"

- ... "On a scale of 1-10 for your children?"

- ... "On a scale of 1-10 for your family?"

- ... "On a scale of 1-10 for Friends?"

- "On a scale of 1-10, how happy and satisfied are you with your time freedom?"

- "Is there anything else about your life here and now that you'd like to share?"

You'll want to write the number that corresponds with each question.

Want some examples from prospects?

- Finances. **3**.
- Career/job/business. **4**.
- Home. **7**.
- Health and fitness. **6**.
- Relationships with partner/spouse: **10**.
- Children. **7**.
- Other family. **5**.
- Friends. **6**.
- Time freedom. **3**.
- Anything else. **6**.

We will need these answers for steps #5 and #6.

Step #5: Identify the Gaps.

We'll have the list of the prospects' dreams on one side of the sheet of paper. On the other side, we'll have the list for the prospects' here and now.

Now, we'll close the gap between the prospects' dreams and their here and now. We will use their own words for closing the gaps.

What do we say?

- "So, clearly there's a gap between where you are here and now and where you want to be."

- "In your description of the "Island of Your Dreams," you said you'd love to: (**Read back what the prospects told you**).
  - "Coach sports in the local community."
  - "Have four children."
  - "A new Ford Explorer with all the bells and whistles."
  - "Large 7-bedroom home on Florida's Cocoa Beach with 8 full baths."
  - "Second home on Lake Ontario with 7-bedrooms and 8 baths."
  - "Travel to Vienna, Austria and San Diego to see the famous zoo."
  - "Mission trips to Haiti."
  - "Travel first class."
  - "Eat healthier."
  - "Exercise more."
  - "Join a gym and hire a personal trainer."
  - "Lose 30 pounds."
  - "Maintain strong relationships with my wife, children, family and friends."
  - "Time freedom to travel at whim without the worry of cost."
  - "Make sure my wife and children have everything they need."

- "Does that sound right? (Let the prospects answer and add to their dreams)."
- "And then here's the Island of the Here and Now. On a scale of 1 to 10, you said (**Read back what the prospects told you**):"
    - "Your finances are a 3."
    - "Your career/job/business is a 4."
    - "Your home is a 7."
    - "Your health and fitness are a 6."
    - "Your relationships with partner/spouse are a 10."
    - "Your relationships with your children are a 7."
    - "Your relationships with other family are a 5."
    - "Your relationships with friends are 6."
    - "Your time freedom is a 3."
    - "And everything else is a 6."
- "Does that sound right to you? (**Let the prospects answer and add to the list**)."
- "So, there's a significant gap between where you are and where you'd like to be."
    - "On a scale of 1 to 10, how important is it for you to get your dream life? (**Wait for their answer**)."
    - "On a scale of 1 to 10, how willing are you to do whatever it takes to get your dream life? (**Wait for their answer**)."

- Whatever their answers for the last two questions, we'll move forward with step #6. It will be very hard for the prospects to deny what they've told you with their own words.

Step #6: Bridge the gaps.

Here is where we will introduce our business presentation.

Sending our prospects to websites, videos, audio files won't be necessary. We will give our prospects a two-minute story for answering all their questions.

Our two-minute story will have all the information for the prospect to make a "yes-decision."

What's not included in a two-minute story?

- Trivia about our compensation plans.
- Information about the corporate offices.
- Data on how our scientists can beat up your scientists.
- Data on how our scientists can beat up your scientists.

Lots of details will bloat the story. A presentation will need only to answer three questions.

What kind of business are you in?

- How much money can I make?
- What do I have to do to earn the money?

Can't believe that three questions could give all the answers for prospects?

- What kind of business are you in? We are in the auto recovery business.

- How much money can I make? You could earn an extra $100,000 a year.

- What do I have to do to earn the money? All you will have to do is steal ten cars a month from one side of town and sell them to us in the same month on this side of town. And then at the end of three months, you will earn an extra $100,000 a year.

Our company doesn't want for any of us to be heading for the "hoosegow big house" (**prison** for all you hicks). So, we'll offer a better way for making money.

- What kind of business are you in? We are in the health and wellness business, which means people drink our products for losing weight and energizing the body.

- How much money can I make? You could earn $100,0000 a year.

- What do I have to do to earn the money? All you have to do is talk 150 people into drinking our products every day. Then you'll earn an extra income of $100,000 a year.

Want another example?

- What kind of business are you in? We are in the organic cleaning business, which means we make homes safe for family and pets from harmful chemicals.

- How much money can I make? You can earn $100,000 a year.

- What do I have to do to earn the money? All you will have to do is get 10 people a month on social media to buy our products every day. At the end of six months, you will begin earning $100,000 a year.

Want one example for our products?

- What kind of products do you have? We are in the healthy coffee business, which means our coffee is caffeine free, tastes great, cost less money and helps you lose weight.

- What can this product do for me? This product will help you lose 20 pounds in 20 days.

- What do I have to do to get the benefits for the product? Drink one cup of our healthy coffee before any meal, and the pounds will start melting away. On the 20th day, you will look at the scales say, "Wow! My belly has shrunk seven inches and I have lost 20 pounds."

So far, our presentation has all the information for our prospects to make a "yes-decision." But the presentation is not interesting enough for holding their attention. We will want to spruce up the presentation by putting it in a story.

People will listen to a story more so than they will listen to a boring fact-filled presentation.

What are the elements of our story? There are ten parts.

1. "Earlier you gave me your top three "here and now problems. <"Here and Now Problem #1"> + <"Here

and Now Problem #2"> + <"Here and Now Problem #3>. Is that right?"

2. "Then you gave me your top three "Dreams." <"Dream #1"> + <"Dream #2"> + <"Dream #3"> + Does that sound right?"

3. "I've got a good story. Takes about two-minutes. It might work for helping you achieve your dreams. It might not. Want to hear it?"

4. Would it be okay if you could + <"A Benefit"> and never have to worry about <"Here and Now Problem #1"> + <"Here and Now Problem #2"> + <"Here and Now Problem #3"> + and going back to work again?"

5. "So, how much money would you need a month, just to cover the basic bills, so you would never have to worry about those three problems and going back to work again?"

6. "Well, you know how most people drink/take/consume/buy..." + <"Product Description #1"> + <"Product Description #2"> + <"Product Description #3>?"

7. "Well, there is a great company called <Name of the Company>, that makes healthy versions/toxin-free versions/lowers... + <"Product Description #1"> + <"Product Description #2"> + <"Product Description #3>."

8. "Now, if you'd never wanted to worry about <"Here and Now Problem #1"> + <"Here and Now Problem #2"> + <"Here and Now Problem #3"> and going back to work again, here's all you'd have to do. Between you

and everybody you know, and everybody they know and everybody they talk to, forever and ever and ever, is to accumulate _____ people drinking our healthy product on a daily basis. Then you would earn an extra $_____ a month."

9. "Now, you don't know how to get ___ people drinking/consuming/using our products every day, but you can learn. You learned how to drive a car, you learned how to use your smartphone. And you can learn a **system** for getting _____ people drinking/ consuming/using our services/products every day."

10. "What's going to be easier for you? To continue with little or no passion for <"Here and Now Problem #1"> + <"Here and Now Problem #2"> + <"Here and Now Problem #3>? Or to learn a system for getting ___ people drinking/consuming/using our products every day and having a career for... <"Dream #1"> + <"Dream #2"> + <"Dream #3"> instead?"

Take the top three "Here and Now Problems" from step #5.

1. Finances.

2. Time-freedom.

3. Job.

Then take the top three Dreams from step #5.

1. A 7-bedroom home on Florida's Cocoa Beach with 8 full baths.

2. A second home on Lake Ontario with 7 bedrooms and 8 baths.

3.   Eating healthier and exercising more with the help of a personal trainer.

Let's add "Here and Now Problems" and "Dreams" to our story for making our story come alive?

- **YOU**: "Earlier you gave me your top three "here and now problems. Finances. Time-freedom. Your job. Is that right?"

- **PROSPECT**: Correct!

- **YOU**: "Then you gave me your top three "Dreams." A 7-bedroom home on Florida's Cocoa Beach with 8 full baths. A second home on Lake Ontario with 7 bedrooms and 8 baths. And Eating healthier and exercising more with the help of a personal trainer. Does that sound right?"

- **PROSPECT**: Right again.

- **YOU**: Well, I've got a good story. Takes about two-minutes. It might work for helping you achieve all your dreams. It might not. Want to hear it?

- **PROSPECT**: Yes!

- **YOU**: Would it be okay if you could energize your body and make big money for it and never have to worry about your finances, time-freedom and going back to your job again?

- **PROSPECT**: Yes!

- **YOU**: How much money would you need a month, just to cover the basic bills, so you would never have to worry about your finances, time-freedom and going back to your job again?

- **PROSPECT**: $10,000 a month.

- **YOU**: Well, you know how most people drink energy products every day?

- **PROSPECT**: Yea, I drink them all the time.

- **YOU**: Well, there's this wonderful company called "Mr. Wonderful" that makes an all-natural energy drink that everybody loves.

- **PROSPECT**: Okay!

- **YOU**: "Now, if you'd never wanted to worry about your finances, time-freedom and going back to your job again? here's all you'd have to do. Between you and everybody you know, and everybody they know and everybody they talk to, forever and ever and ever, is to accumulate 400 people drinking our healthy product daily. Then you would earn an extra $10,000 a month."

- **YOU**: Now, you don't know how to get 400 people drinking our all-natural herbal energy product every day. But you can learn. You learned how to drive a car. You learned how to use a smartphone. And you certainly can learn a **system** for getting 400 people drinking our all-natural herbal energy product every day.

- **YOU**: So, what's going to be easier for you? To continue with little or no passion for your finances, lack of time-freedom and going back to work again? Or to learn a **system** for getting 400 people drinking our healthy all-natural herbal energy product, and having a career for getting you..."

1. A Seven-bedroom home on Florida's Cocoa Beach with 8 full baths,

2. A second home on Lake Ontario with 7 bedrooms and 8 baths, and

3. Eating healthier and exercising more with the help of a personal trainer instead?

- **PROSPECT**: It's going to be easier to learn a system.

Want one more example?

Let's list our top three "Here and Now" problems.

1. Home,

2. Friends,

3. Finances.

Now, let's list the top three "Dreams."

1. A new Ford Explorer.

2. A vacation home in the Caribbean islands every month.

3. Putting your wife through school without debt.

We have everything we will need for telling our story.

- **YOU**: "Earlier you gave me your top three "here and now problems. Your home. Friends. Finances?" Is that right?

- **PROSPECT**: Correct!

- **YOU**: "Then you gave me your top three "Dreams." A new Ford Explorer. A vacation home in the Caribbean islands every month. And putting your wife through school without debt. Does that sound right?"

- **PROSPECT**: Right again.

- **YOU**: I've got a good story. Takes about two-minutes. It might work for helping you achieve all your dreams. It might not. Want to hear it?

- **PROSPECT**: Sounds good to me.

- **YOU**: Would it be okay if you could make more money part-time than you make full-time and never have to worry about your home, friends, finances, and going back to your job again?

- **PROSPECT**: Of course.

- **YOU**: So, how much money would you need a month, just to cover the basic bills, so you would never have to worry about your home, friends, finances, and going back to your job again?

- **PROSPECT**: $6,000 a month.

- **YOU**: Well, you know how most people use laundry cleaners, hand soaps, floor cleaners and dishwashing soap every day?

- **PROSPECT**: Who doesn't?

- **YOU**: Well, there's this great company called "Mr. Wonderful" that makes toxin-free versions of laundry cleaners, hand soaps, floor cleaners and dishwashing soap that all people love.

- **PROSPECT**: Okay!

- **YOU**: Now, if you never wanted to worry about home, friends, finances, and going back to your job, here's all you'd have to do. Between you and everybody you know, and everybody they talk to, forever and ever and ever, is eventually accumulate 240 people using our toxin-free and environmentally safe products every day on a regular basis. Then you would earn an extra $6,000 a month.

- **YOU**: Now, FIRST NAME, you don't know how to get 240 people to use our environmentally friendly products every day. But you can learn. You learned how to use to use a computer. You learned how to navigate the internet. And you certainly can learn a **system** for getting 240 people using our environmentally safe and toxin-free products every day.

- **YOU**: So, what's going to be easier for you? To continue with little or no passion for your home, lack of friends, finances, and going back to your job again? Or to learn a **system** for getting 240 people using our toxin-free and environmentally safe products every day, and having a career for getting you...

  1. "A new Ford Explorer."

  2. "A vacation home in the Caribbean islands every month."

  3. "And putting your wife through school without debt instead?"

- **PROSPECT**: It's going to be easier to learn a system.

Have we answered all three questions?

1. What kind of business are you in?
2. How much money can I make?
3. What do I have to do to earn the money?

The answer is "Yes."

Have we given a presentation by telling it in a great story? Yes.

The best part? Our presentation will take only two-minutes. Who does not like a two-minute presentation?

We will need to know how many people it will take for a person in our business to make money? You will want to keep a calculator nearby.

Here's how we'll find the answer.

Our company will pay us a $25.00 bonus for every $100 in products purchased a month.

- So, figure the bonus amount paid by your company for every $100 a month in purchased products. Then you will need to write it down.
- Our prospect has told us he will need $10,000 a month for covering his basic bills.
- So, we will divide $10,000 by $25.00 and arrive at 400 people.
- Our prospect will need 400 customers purchasing $100 worth of products a month for him to make $10,000 a month.

- If the prospect will need $6,000 a month, we will divide $6,000 by $25.00 and arrive at 240 people.

It's time for you to take the ten elements of the story and fill in the blanks for creating your own two-minute story.

Step #7: The Close.

We will close with one question and three backup questions.

Our one question for closing?

"How would you like to get started?"

Here is where our skills for handling objections could come in handy the most. If the prospects have any objections, they will ask them here. Answer the objections with honesty and briefly.

For the one-question close, we will ask the question and be quiet and wait for the prospects to answer. We will keep silent even if the silence is longer than anticipated. I've waited as much as five minutes.

If the prospects do ask for more information, then we will use our three back-up questions.

1. What would you like to know first?

2. What would you like to know next?

3. What would you like to do next?

We will answer the first two questions with honest answers. The third question throws the ball back into the prospect's court.

Step 8: The Referral.

What happens if your prospect doesn't buy or join? Ask for a referral.

Here's the formula for referrals.

"I know you said you were not interested, but would you do me a favor? I'm looking for people who <**have this problem**> and want to fix it. Do you know anybody?"

- "I know you said you were not interested, but would you do me a favor? I'm looking for people who hate to commute to work and would rather work out of their homes. Do you know anybody?"

- "I know you said you were not interested, but would you do me a favor? I'm looking for people who hate their bosses and would love to be their own boss. Do you know anybody?"

- "I know you said you were not interested, but would you do me a favor? I'm looking for people stretched for time spending with their spouse and children. Do you know anybody?"

- "I know you said you were not interested, but would you do me a favor? I'm looking for people who will retire soon and would like to double their retirement pension. Do you know anybody?"

- "I know you said you were not interested, but would you do me a favor? I'm looking for mothers with stretch marks and don't want them. Do you know anybody?"

- "I know you said you were not interested, but would you do me a favor? I'm looking for people who have two jobs but would prefer one job. Do you know anybody?"

- "I know you said you were not interested, but would you do me a favor? I'm looking for people who want to diet but can't find the time to exercise. Do you know anybody?"

- "I know you said you were not interested, but would you do me a favor? I'm looking for people who have a lot of credit card debt and want to pay it off early. Do you know anybody?"

- "I know you said you were not interested, but would you do me a favor? I'm looking for people with electric bills who would rather pay a lower rate. Do you know anybody?"

LinkedIn for Network Marketing has never been easier than it is for you now. I've made all the hard work easier for you. Learn, practice and enjoy the lessons taught by this book.

I hope seeing you all on the better side of success.

Dale

About the Author

Dale Moreau has been in Network Marketing since 2008 and has been a keynote speaker, trainer and mentor on how to make Network Marketing work on social media. He has effectively gotten "yes" decisions from prospects on LinkedIn and laid the pathway for others to follow.

To contact Dale, call him at 210-478-6975

Or, contact him through his website: dalemoreau.net

Manufactured by Amazon.ca
Bolton, ON

12923970R00138